identIty

CONNECT WITH YOUR AUTHENTIC BEING

Disclaimer

All the information, techniques, skills and concepts contained within this publication are of the nature of general comment only and are not in any way recommended as individual advice. The intent is to offer a variety of information to provide a wider range of choices now and in the future, recognising that we all have widely diverse circumstances and viewpoints.

Should any reader choose to make use of the information contained herein, this is their decision, and the contributors (and their companies), authors and publishers do not assume any responsibilities whatsoever under any condition or circumstances. It is recommended that the reader obtain their own independent advice.

First Edition 2021

Copyright © 2021 by Alexander Gil

All rights reserved. No part of this publication may be reproduced, stored in a retrieval system, or transmitted in any form or by any means, electronic, mechanical, photocopying, recording or otherwise, without the prior written permission from the publisher.

A catalogue record for this book is available from the National Library of Australia

Title: Identity- Connect with your authentic being
ISBN(s): 978-1-925471-58-8
Author: Alexander Gil

Published with support by Author Express
www.AuthorExpress.com
publish@authorexpress.com

For George and Esme

CONTENTS

PREFACE

CHAPTER 1: IDENTITY — 1

CHAPTER 2: THE 3 P's — 5
- Purpose — 6
- Poise — 7
- Personality — 9

CHAPTER 3: IDENTITY CRISIS — 13
- Digital Dementia — 17
- Digital Deduction — 18

CHAPTER 4: WHO ARE YOU? — 19
- Spiral of Despair — 21
- Dopamine Production Center — 22
- Your Why — 23
- Positive Psychology — 26
- Fulfillment Techniques — 27
- Identity Techniques — 29

CHAPTER 5: EMOTIONS — 31
- Automatic Negative Thoughts (ANT's) — 33
- Positive Mental Attitude (PMA) — 33
- The Three areas of the Brain — 36
- Emotional Reframing Techniques — 36

CHAPTER 6: EMOTIONAL TRIGGERS — 39
- Grounding Tools — 50
- Diffusion Tools — 51
- Thought Tools — 52

CHAPTER 7: EMOTIONAL WAVE	55
• Life Principle	57
• Stages of Learning	58
• Grounding Techniques	59
CHAPTER 8: THE 4 A's	61
• Authenticity	62
- The Five Stages of Self-Deception	65
- Techniques for Achieving Authenticity	68
- Questions to help you reflect on your Authenticity	70
• Accountability	72
- Techniques for better Accountability	76
• Adversity	76
- Plus, Minus, Equals mindset	79
- Techniques or Tackling Adversity	84
• Attitude	85
- Layers to your Attitude	87
CHAPTER 9: BOUNDARIES	91
• Time	94
• Money	95
CHAPTER 10: THE HEALTHY ADULT	99
• Self-Awareness	104
• Self-Compassion	106
• Belief	109
THE FINAL WORD	113
ABOUT THE AUTHOR	117
ACKNOWLEDGMENTS	118
REFERENCES	120
THE ULTIMATE LIST OF EMOTIONS	122

PREFACE

This book will help bring insight into learning who you are, why you operate the way you do and give you the reflection tools to max-out your life. It raises questions that will help you flourish and offer perspective to living a fulfilled life. The best way to ingest it is to go through and figure out which parts resonate with you. Treat this like a buffet. Take from it what you need by highlighting, underlining and annotating.

Each time you pick up the book from where you left off, you should re-read the highlighted parts, so by the end of this process, you will know who you are and how to go out into the world and be the light. This is how I was taught to process books.

I would highly recommend having a pen and pad to answer some of the existential questions that are asked throughout. Feel free to stop and reflect upon them.

CHAPTER 1
IDENTITY

In the social jungle of human existence, there is no feeling of being alive without a sense of identity.

- Erik Erikson

CHAPTER 1: IDENTITY

- ✓ What is identity?
- ✓ Where does it come from?
- ✓ How can you learn what it is?
- ✓ What is your identity?
- ✓ Do you know who you are?

Our identity is as unique as each single snowflake. Our fingertips, our eyes, our hearts, are all slightly different than from any other human's, but do we truly know what makes us different?

Who are you is one of the most commonly asked questions in the world, and it could have many different variations, such as:

- ✓ What is your name?
- ✓ Who are you?
- ✓ What do you do?
- ✓ What are you into?
- ✓ What is your story?
- ✓ What do you stand for?
- ✓ Tell me about yourself.

Your identity is who you are. It's your beliefs, values and why you do what you do. It can be influenced by your environment (the where and when) and behaviour (the what).

CHAPTER 1: Identity

The meaning and literal translation of Identity is:

/aɪˈdɛntəti/ (pl. identities) noun

[countable, uncountable] (abbreviation ID) 1. Who or what someone or something is.

[countable, uncountable] 2. The characteristics, feelings, or beliefs that distinguish people from others.

If you breakdown who or what someone is to a granular level, you're literally a merger of all your habits. Have you ever taken audit of them? You've probably checked your bank balance, so why wouldn't you take an audit of your daily habits? They ripple out weekly, monthly and yearly to how you do anything and everything.

Your skin sheds every seven years, so you're literally a new person then, than from who you were seven years ago. But what has changed? You carry on through life with many subconscious habits, such as checking your social media accounts, juggling between them to see if you've been approved, connected with or liked. These days, everyone is addicted to endorphin-based approvals. Simon Sinek has interestingly stated that people go to Instagram for social acceptance, Facebook for connecting, Tinder for love, gaming for prestige/status, and recently, Tik Tok for validation, which is a basic human need.

Nowadays we are so distracted by notifications people do not fully connect with themselves.

CHAPTER 2
THE 3 P'S

Adventure isn't hanging a rope off the side of a mountain. Adventure is an attitude that we must apply to the day-to-day obstacles of life – facing new challenges, seizing new opportunities, testing our resources against the unknown and, in the process, discovering our own unique potential.

- John Amatt

CHAPTER 2: THE 3 P'S

Now that you know the meaning of identity, I want to propose the three P's to you. These are deep-rooted power points that contribute to your identity, and you can take audit of them straight away. They're areas you should actively seek answers to, as they're the building blocks of a healthy human. You're not the person you once were many years ago, so who is the person you will be in years to come? When you break these three sections down, they can help you identify who you are as you question what your actions have been until now.

PURPOSE

If a man hasn't discovered something that he will die for,
he isn't fit to live.
-Dr Martin Luther King

We now know that certainty crystallises purpose. I'm sure that every beautiful human on this earth wasn't born to merely be tolerant or entertain their life away. As Malcolm X once said, "That which you do not hate, you will eventually tolerate". So, are you tolerating life?

Once you crystallise your purpose, it amplifies your identity, creating certainty in knowing who you are. Your purpose is your mission statement. You heal yourself by healing others. No single human gets through childhood unscathed, so you constantly work on your future by healing your past. The secret is that you must move forward. My purpose is to help as many humans as possible by sharing stories, giving perspective and being a great listener. Sometimes people just want to be validated and heard.

CHAPTER 2: The 3 P's

Also, the male and female brain work differently and have different purposes. As Dave Ramsey, a personal finance advisor, says, "Men look for achievement, whereas women look for meaningful relationships".

Your purpose could be something like caring for the ill, looking after children, finding the cure for a disease or being an Olympic athlete. Whatever your intention is, make it a dominating thought and part of your Identity. To know your purpose is to know your passion. To know your passion is to know your heart. To know your heart is to connect with your internal electrical system. To know your system is to know who you are.

Pablo Picasso once said, "The meaning of life is to find your gift. The purpose of life is to give it away". To figure out your purpose and gain perspective, seek the advice of the people in your life who are neither unloving critics nor uncritical loves, but those you trust and admire.

POISE

You are what you repeatedly do.
Excellence is not an event; it is a habit.
-Aristotle

The second power tool is your poise, which is how you hold yourself. It's the outer radiation of your shell. We are all spiritual beings having an earthly experience. There is a direct correlation between how you feel and how your body presents itself, which is why this is so key.

What is your posture? How do you hold yourself? Do you keep your head high and strong, with your crown upright? I believe that in order to prevent the correct emotions from being blocked, you should walk around with your chest full of oxygen, collar bone stretched out, filled with pride. Try being like this for a week, and notice the difference. I did it as an experiment and couldn't help smiling!
Your physical actions express your mental attitudes. Having your eyes down and being hunched over depicts an unsure mind.

People are attracted to clarity, consistency and certainty. Jordan Peterson, in *12 rules for life*, says, "If you slump around, with the same bearing that characterizes a defeated lobster, people will assign you with a lower status, and the low counter you share with crustaceans, sitting at the base of your brain, will assign you a low dominance number. Then your brain will not produce as much serotonin".

The need to take dominance of your poise is a key to your success. Being slumped over will not only make you feel more hurt, anxious and weak, but also impact what you attract in your life. A healed, confident and strong composure will attract higher vibrations. Nobody wants to be at the bottom of the pecking order, and when you take ownership for your shell, you make the choice to elevate yourself.

CHAPTER 2: The 3 P's

PERSONALITY

The greatest revolution of our generation is in the discovery that human beings, by changing the inner attitudes of their minds, can change the outer aspects of their lives.
-William James, Psychologist/Philosopher

Another part of identity is personality, which is your personal reality. So who are you going to be? What actions do you want to take, and what legacy do you want to leave?

Character is integral to your personality. I've been spending a lot of time alone lately to understand my soul and body, and how I can connect better with myself. In the book *Personality Plus* by Florence Littauer, she defines four types of personalities as choleric, melancholy, sanguine and phlegmatic. The popular sanguine loves fun and excitement, while the over-achieving melancholy strives for perfection in everything and is orderly. The powerful choleric is a natural leader who's always right and knows everything, and the peaceful phlegmatic is laidback, happy and reconciled in life.

Growing up with a mum with mental health challenges, I've always been intrigued with personality. My mum has lived a life battling her own inner critic and can be a difficult person to be around, as at times she lets her fleeting emotions rule her.

Brendan Burchard, a high-performance coach, has written about release techniques and leaving emotions at the door. Successful people, or those who live in abundance and have a meaningful life, do not let their emotions act as dictators, but indicators.

Following through on actions long after the emotion has left, is the definition of character.

Character is built from trust within yourself and leads to self-esteem, which is an internal contract to follow through long after the emotion is gone.

I once saw Anthony Laye speak at a business seminar about how you should turn up in the world, which he broke up into three parts:

1. How should you turn up for yourself?
2. Who is the person you need to be?
3. How do you need to turn up for the people you love?

I loved this breakdown, as these three questions are a great principle to live by.

The best coaches in the world agree that *your character is your choice*. Optimism can be learned. Life happens through you, not to you.

The Fogg Behaviour Model is a perfect example of this:
Behaviour = habits
B = MAT (motivation, ability, trigger)

CHAPTER 2: The 3 P's

In essence, your *motivation* comes from your behaviour, so you must have the *ability* to exhibit the behaviour before being *triggered* or prompted to. If one of the elements is missing, the *behaviour* won't happen.

Now that you've reflected on your three Power P's, coagulate who you are, and connect with your authentic being by answering these questions:

- ✓ What is your personal reality?
- ✓ What is your poise?
- ✓ What is your purpose?

CHAPTER 3
IDENTITY CRISIS

*Strength does not come from physical capacity.
It comes from an indomitable will.*

- Mahatma Gandhi

CHAPTER 3: IDENTITY CRISIS

I want to speak to you with candour, if that's okay. This book will expose some of my vulnerabilities, but the whole purpose is to share my learnings and enable you to grow your mindset. To believe and dream.

I've have had some real adversity in life, where I didn't respond to situations in the way I should have. I just reacted, rather than thinking about what results my actions might cause. I didn't know any better at the time and was not equipped with this knowledge that you are about to learn.

Would I go back and change anything from the past? Absolutely not! I've sat with my regrets and seen them as an opportunity to re-greet the past and learn from it. To understand and grow from it. I believe you need to have a breakdown to have a breakthrough. It enables you to self-discover and understand yourself, but also find purpose.

Have you ever had an identity crisis before? I'm about to give you a perspective shift that you may never be able to un-see.

In response to someone asking who you are, you might say, for example, "I'm Joe Bloggs, and I'm a consultant". But have you ever stepped back to question why you do this? What made you get into your career? Why you're still there?

Information has been passed down to you like the elders would have done centuries ago, but how much are you questioning? Back in the day, about seventy years ago, it was rare to go to university to get a degree and then a job. Nowadays, it's a given. We celebrate by wearing

CHAPTER 3: Identity Crisis

a weird hat and a funeral-looking gown. I mean, come on. Why is this a tradition? For my graduation, I had a huge spot on my forehead, and I'd never had one there before, so it must have been my nerves due to wearing my Darth Vader crossed with a *Blackadder* costume.

You've been trained like a monkey in a circus. You go to school, study hard, receive good grades and get into a good university. As Steve Jobs once said, if you want to please everyone, you should sell ice cream. I'm just here to highlight some truths.

Robert Kiyosaki, author of *Rich Dad Poor Dad*, says, "It's an antiquated system, studying subjects you will never use, preparing you for a world that no longer exists". Study hard at university to get a degree and a good job, so then you can get plugged into a system of *trading your time for money*. Have you ever thought about that? Bear in mind, this way of living your life may put added pressure on your relationships, mental health and body. And once you finish your prison sentence, depending on which country you live in, you might get seventy pounds a week or receive your superannuation (a better system, in my opinion).

Why do we not question the system? Where are the days when we would trade our values with others? Why are we not all released from this practice?

The honest truth is that not everyone can break free from this process, as otherwise the world would stop rotating. Polliwog!

I believe in fulfilment, positive psychology and a state of flourishing and accomplishment, but any person who works five days and lives two, in my eyes, is tolerating life. We coast through our lives, never really enjoying our days. What are you tolerating? John Maxwell said it well.

"Most people don't live their life; they just accept their life".

This reflection has made me question why we continue on like this. Is it due to the committee of 'they'? You know who I'm talking about. *They* say this, or *they* say that. I had a chat with my Dad and Step Mum about how I'd joined the glasses group, and that I loved them. Did they add character to my face? Hell, yeah! And *I chose* to be optimistic. Was there anything I could do about my body aging and my eyes deteriorating? No, a mentor once taught me that age wrinkles the body, but quitting wrinkles the soul.

So as I spoke with my parents, they asked if I wore my glasses all the time, and I replied, "I wear them as much as I can". They let me know that I shouldn't, because it would cause my eyes to deteriorate, so I asked them which specialist they got their information from. As they both looked at each other, stunned, I asked, "Was this the committee of *they*?" We laughed, but in all seriousness, we're evolving into an age where an electronic device informs us how to think and what to do on a daily basis. And we're addicted to it.

What are we not questioning?

Have you ever lost your phone? Did you pat down your pockets and check your jacket? It gets even worse when you're in public. You need to sit with that feeling in your gut. The loss. It's even worse if you were intoxicated the night before, as your memory isn't optimal, due to the alcoholic effects on your brain.

We're now so dependent and attached to this device, but still unaware of how much. Can you feel the emotional release, the pleasure, when you see a notification from Facebook, Instagram, Twitter, Tik Tok or

CHAPTER 3: Identity Crisis

Snapchat? This triggers the same endorphins that are released in drug and substance abusers.

There are many people behind those apps whose sole purpose is to make sure there's user engagement. There are many subtleties we're unaware of. Have you ever stopped to question how they're a lot like slot machines? Only these images never come to a stop.

Nowadays, there's so much information on the internet with no accountability, that it's breeding digital dementia. In my research, I looked for proof as to who backs the information I'm receiving. Check this out:

One of the greatest leaders of all time in my eyes was Abraham Lincoln. His mentor passed down to him some great skills, and his burning desire to abolish slavery. This came at great cost, but Abe taught us many things, such as how "most people are about as happy as they make up their minds to be".

People use search engines in their quest for clarity. However, there's no accountability as to how factual the results are, so they miss the boat and believe whatever they read as the truth. It leads to unconnected humans, as this way of seeking information clogs the natural pathways for bonding. Google is a search engine, not a research engine.

If there's one thing you get from this book, I hope it's to question where the information comes from. Jim Qwik, a brain coach who helps people with mental expansion, wrote a book entitled *Limitless*, in which he coined the term Digital Deduction. It's the idea that technology is now thinking for us, so we don't have to. He quotes Rony Zarom, founder of Newrow, who says, "In a digital-first world, where millennials obtain all their answers to problems at the click of a mouse or swipe of a finger, the reliance on technology to solve every question confuses people's perception of their own knowledge and intelligence. And that reliance may well lead to overconfidence and poor decision-making". Jim goes on to also talk about digital dementia, distraction and deluge. This relates to a subconscious reliance and the harvesting of an identity crisis, as people post a different lifestyle online than the one they live in real life, so they become confused about who they are. We're now in a *filter fantasy* era.

To enable your future, you need to be accountable for your own actions. It's hard, but, in this process, you learn who you are. I will help guide you by providing you with a few techniques that helped me.

An identity crisis is a wakeup call to take your life by the reins and to be in control of your outcome through focus, knowing who you are, understanding your *Why* and having determination. After going through real adversity in my life, which I will touch on later, I had an identity crisis. But after embracing the three P's, I took back my life from the oppressive delusion of my victim mentality, to lead a flourishing life.

Your calling is your purpose. Be compassionate, love others, take your eyes off yourself and serve one another.

CHAPTER 4
WHO ARE YOU?

The world makes way for the man who knows where he is going.

- Ralph Waldo Emerson

CHAPTER 4: WHO ARE YOU?

Take some time now, and write down the answer to the question, "Who are you?" This exercise may be invasive for some or a booster for others, as well as a turning point.

There are many elements that go into understanding how to answer this question, but knowing who you are is integral to your future. If you're consumed with being entertained, then you may be distracting yourself until the point when you have an epiphany, which might take the form of a breakdown. It could also be a mid-life or quarter-life crisis.

This next generation, who are dependent on their smart devices, may find out they're now the servant to them, and not the other way around. This is evident when people cover up emotions by suppressing them with electronics and wind up going into a downward spiral of despair.

CHAPTER 4: Who Are You?

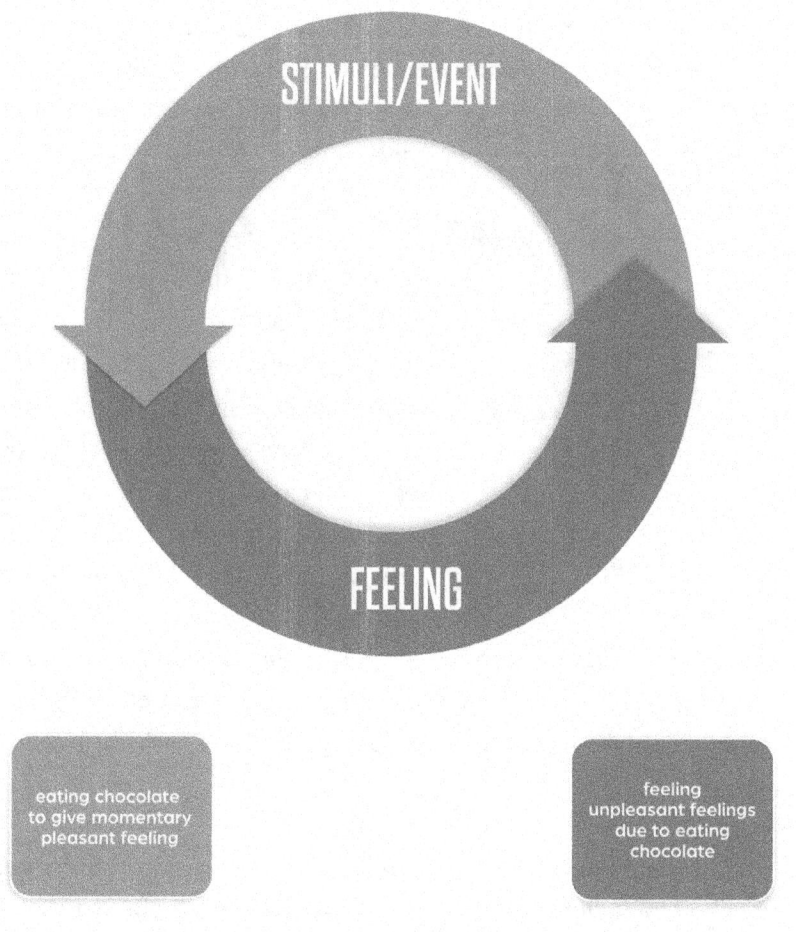

An example of this is: Eat chocolate – get fat – eat more chocolate for the momentary endorphins – repeat the process.

This model can be compared to the endorphin-based society we live in.

Dopamine, located in the middle of the brain, is released when a good feeling occurs. It then transfers to the frontal lobe, the neocortex, known as the pleasure centre. When the dopamine is released, your brain cells scream at you, "Do it again! That felt good!" The more dopamine that's released, the more you want it. Like a rat with a pellet, your brain trains you to pick up the phone, as there could be another dopamine dump. This is where addiction comes from. Your mobile produces the same amount of dopamine as nicotine and alcohol. To break this habit, you need to replace it.

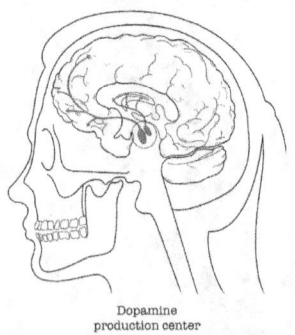

Dopamine production center

The neocortex is the newer part of the brain that's able to communicate the message, as this is where your translation abilities come from, while the limbic part is where feelings come from. Society is unconscious of this addiction. Another great question to ask yourself is, *What are my emotional drivers?*

Furthermore, a big part of what plays into understanding who you are is knowing your Why. It's your burning desire, the root of living in discomfort and the reason you act the way you do. It's what drives your future.

There are often layers to your burning desire. Your Why can be your motivation for going out of your comfort zone, such as your family, your kids or a better life. A lot of people never question what their Why is. Do you go to work? Do you tap into why you do? You're trading your time for money, to then get commodities and provide yourself and your family with food, water, shelter and electricity.

CHAPTER 4: Who Are You?

Your Why is a personal thing that you need to sit on and ponder over. A great question to multilayer this is, *Who are you performing for?*

To go even deeper, ask yourself what your values are. Have you ever written them out? You're not taught in school to figure out what they are and live by them. People graduate with a grade, when they should graduate with an improved self-image. You're asked *what* you want to do rather than *who* do you want to be.

Often, when you don't live through your values, you spiral into the self-deception diagram I speak of in chapter eight. A way to ponder on this is to ask yourself, *What brings me fulfilment?*

Personally, my values are time, respectfulness, family, health, kindness and eudaimonia (well-being). Of course, there's also love and spirituality.

**

You need to face your fear, and you can do that by breaking it down. Know that you're David against Goliath, and I believe in you. Fear of rejection can stem from childhood. However, as Ichiro Kishimi, a Japanese psychologist and philosopher, cleverly says, "No matter what has occurred in your life up to this point, it should have no bearing at all on how you live from now on". Therefore, you can address rejection by:

- ✓ Knowing your Why
- ✓ Knowing your Identity
- ✓ Being Prepared

We've already covered the first two, so now let's talk about preparation.

I mean this in terms of being a fighter or a dancer. These dedicated individuals are built off-stage but recognised for their performance. The practice of mindset is one you should *nourish, encourage* and *practice*.

Due to society's instant gratification undertone, a lot of people don't believe in practicing to get good at something. There are even misconceptions. I'll use the example of PokemonGo. This app was perceived as an overnight success and broke all records, with over ten million downloads in the first week. Little did people know that John Hanke, the creator, had been practicing and working on this with patience. The app was twenty years in the making. Starting in 1996, while he was still a student, John co-created the very first massive multiplayer online game (MMOG) called Meridian 59. It went through many iterations, such as in 2004, when Google bought Keyhole, and with John's help, turned it into what is now Google Earth. This is when John decided to focus on creating GPS-based games.

In 2010 he launched Niantic Labs as a start-up funded by Google to create a game that would layer on maps. In 2014, Google and the Pokémon Company teamed up for an April Fool's Day joke that allowed viewers to find Pokémon creatures on Google maps.

John raised twenty-five million from Google, Nintendo, the Pokémon Company and other investors, from December 2015 to February 2016, and grew a team of over forty people to launch Pokémon Go in the U.S.A., Australia and New Zealand. After its launch, Nintendo's share price rose to twelve billion dollars. John achieved his success by focusing on his next level up, with each iteration being another practice run.

CHAPTER 4: Who Are You?

Did you know that Michael Jordan was cut from his basketball team when he was in school? So what do you think he did? Initially, his brother was better than he was, but Michael made a commitment to his practice and consistently followed through, even when his emotion wasn't running high.

Tiger Woods wasn't always a great golfer. The Williams sisters weren't born champion tennis players. Everybody starts from somewhere, but it was a commitment to practicing that helped them shine. I believe that knowing your Why and your values, and acting in line with them, will build momentum and help you remain dedicated to practicing your skills, as well as improving your integrity and self-esteem. It's in the consistency of practice where you'll flourish. *A champion is recognised in the ring but made in the training.*

The best time to start is now.

You should avoid quitting, as it becomes a habit, just like winning. You can't stop a quitter from quitting, and you cannot stop a winner from winning. The people who look for get-rich-quick schemes will always be on the hunt for the next one, and unfortunately will never follow through, as they don't practice patience. These individuals are lazy to their core with a something-for-nothing pattern of thinking.

All great things come to those who wait.

Chinese bamboo takes five years to grow into its potential. When you look at it within its first few years of growth, you can't see anything above ground. But as you water and fertilize the seemingly empty soil every day, tremendous growth begins to happen beneath the surface. The bamboo is building its root system, which you can think of as your *belief, attitude and mindset.* The bamboo plant spreads its strong roots and obtains the necessary water and nutrients for its special showcase. In the fifth year, after it's built its root network, the bamboo tree will then skyrocket into the air. It bursts with life and grows eighty feet tall within six weeks.

This analogy shows that through *grit* and *faith*, you will get there. You must give everything time, but it's important to commit. If you don't quit, you will make it.

I was once somebody who would start new projects and not commit to patience and improving my skills. We all have a friend who gets into a new hobby and goes all in. Then a few months down the line, they're onto the next thing. This mindset doesn't harvest fulfilment. It harbours *destination disease.*

Fulfilment is a key contributor to who you are. A fulfilled person is able to share their energy with others and shed light on their pathway. We were born with two ears, two eyes and one mouth for a reason. When you're fulfilled and know who you are, then you listen to others more. Dale Carnegie talks about the 101 foundations of people skills and how you have to actually care about others.

Martin Seligman, director of the Penn Positive Psychology Center, coined the term 'positive psychology' in the nineties and adopted some eastern and western ways to talk about a different outlook on life. Certain words that arose were *flourish, thrive* and *fulfillment*. He also talks about building a robust Losada ration (more positive thoughts than negative). I will talk more about Seligman's breakdown later.

**

CHAPTER 4: Who Are You?

When was the last time you felt you were thriving or flourishing? If you're having trouble, here are little hacks you can do to max-out your life

Fulfilment Techniques

1. Brush your teeth with your other hand.
   This helps activate the indentation in your brain, the corpus callosum, that connects the left and right side.

2. Practice mindful eating.
   Take an item of food, such as a peanut, and look at it for a minute. Then smell it for a minute before placing it in your mouth for a minute. Crunch the peanut for a minute and then swallow. This practice can be repeated and teaches you fulfilment and appreciation.

3. Set goals, and delay your gratification in getting there.
   In regard to the question *Who are you*, I would love to leave you with my adapted quote. Dale Carnegie says, "You can't grow yourself, if you don't know yourself". My adaptation is, "What you see, you conceive, and what you believe, you achieve".

Be conscious about what you conceive, and trust in your journey. We're all on this earth for a purpose. We own our life enterprise. We're the CEOs who answer to our stakeholders, so what are the steps you will take to increase your self equity? What are you choosing to believe and adopt as your own mentality? You must have the courage if you're going to act outwardly what you believe inwardly. *We often judge others on their actions, and ourselves on our thoughts*. So push through the fear, and act courageously.

You must identify your belief system (BS), and understand that what you conceive you can achieve. But be consistent with your practicing, and fight through the emotions now that you understand how they travel to the frontal lobe. You've got this!

**

Aristotle said that every virtue is a mean between the extremes of excess and deficiency. Some people say they are lucky. Darren Hardy, in *The Compound Effect*, broke down the formula for getting lucky:

Preparation (personal growth) + Attitude (belief/mindset) + Opportunity (luck) + Action (doing something about it) = Luck.

Preparation is the amount of personal growth you've accumulated. The fact that you're reading this book is an indicator that you want to improve your life.

Attitude comes from your belief system, and according to Carol Dweck in her book *Mindset*, belief is the correlating factor that will influence, maximise and impact attitude. I believe this part is the key to luck, and I'll discuss belief later on.

Opportunity is a good thing coming your way. Action is then to act on the opportunity. We can often get so caught up in our own head, that we don't act upon opportunities. Knowing a thought can't beat a thought, you realise taking action becomes easier. The more you train yourself to act first and think second, and to trust your gut, the more you will get out of life. Your intuition is the best gift. So, are you committing yourself to following your gut, practicing and taking action, or are you committed to being average?

CHAPTER 4: Who Are You?

Identity Techniques

These are some techniques that will help you figure out who you are.

- ✓ Meditate while concentrating on your breath
- ✓ Write out your values
- ✓ Write down your full name one-hundred times
- ✓ Live through your values
- ✓ Know that you feel fear, and act anyway
- ✓ Know your Why
- ✓ Know your Identity

CHAPTER 5
EMOTIONS

Although many of us think of ourselves as thinking creatures that feel, biologically we are feeling creatures that think.

- Dr Jilo Bolte Taylor, Neuroscientist

CHAPTER 5: EMOTIONS

I full-heartedly believe that to know who you are, you need to work with your emotions. At the end of the day, we're human and have the most advanced brain on the planet. But it's running on old software, and biologically, we keep advancing. To think that 150 years ago, people had been enslaved is mind boggling. When you say someone is another race, what do you mean by that? We are all one race; *the human race*.

Back to emotions. Here I want to give a big shout-out to Noble and Kathy Gibbens, pioneering teachers in this field who've mentored me through a great season of my life by giving me perspective. In the back of this book, I've also included a whole list of emotions for you to learn, reference, add to your lexicon and name. Vocabulary is a key skill to foster when working with your emotions. Unfortunately, this old software between your ears sometimes battles you, and you might think you are your thoughts. Your brain is like Windows 95 operating in a technologically advanced world. When did you last do a software update? The beauty of it is that it's malleable. I'm about to share with you how to alter your thoughts, so you have a mind-shift.

If you were to follow your emotions, you wouldn't get the outcome you desired, and on your deathbed, would have regrets. In Dr Anthony Campolo's study of fifty people over the age of ninety-five who were asked what they would do differently if given the opportunity to live life over again, the main three answers were: *reflect more, risk more and do more that will live on*. Most people crave comfort and safety, so what will you risk more and reflect more on, before you have regrets?

CHAPTER 5: Emotions

Your brain is hardwired negatively and has automatic negative thoughts (ANTs), as Dr Daniel Amen defines them, and you need to crush your ants.

It's important to know when a thought is a thought, like an emotion is an emotion. Thoughts are the language of the brain. Emotions are the language of the body. How much power you give that thought will define how long you could be on that emotional rollercoaster. The reason I'm talking about thoughts and emotions at the same time is because a thought has to run through the emotion centre to then reach the thinking part of your brain. A rollercoaster can be an enjoyable ride full of ebbs and flows, of excitements, unknowns, and thrills, but if you're in a state of panic, then it will not be enjoyable.

It's important to be aware of your emotions when making decisions. If you're feeling sad, then you're more likely to anticipate failure and avoid risk. But if you're happy, there's a good possibility that you'll disregard the risk and go for it. You must take note of how you're feeling.

According to Naval Ravikant, "Happiness is a choice that you make and a skill you develop". You may think, *Here we go. Another conversation about how we can think our way into happiness.* Yes, it is. Napoleon Hill's book, *Think and Grow Rich*, is not about *making* yourself rich, but about *thinking* it into being. A positive mental attitude (PMA) can be a challenge. However, as somebody who was consumed with darkness, I want to share some light: you have a choice.

In 2016, I was T-boned off a scooter going 60 kmp/h down the middle lane, while returning home from the cinema. I was thrown ten feet and developed a concussion. The Uber driver was apologetic at the time and said he would do what I preferred, so I said I wanted the bike to be serviced and checked out, as part of it had concaved towards the engine.

Once I returned home, I realised my body had entered a state of shock. My legs wouldn't stop shaking, and my chin followed suit. It was a surreal moment. I turned the heating on and tried to calm my brain.

The next day at work, my back started to hurt, and I had to have a standing desk for several months. But I continued living as normally as I could, not understanding emotion and how it can hook you and highjack your state of mind, much like a caught fish. The difference is that we're in control of our emotions, actions and state of mind, but I wasn't aware of this at the time.

Continuing life while the Uber driver acted, in my opinion, inhumane by changing his story about the event, refusing to pay and not answering my calls, was difficult. My mental attitude wasn't one of positivity. Each day on my walk to work, I would weep and wasn't sure why. Being male, I was brought up with the toxic masculinity mindset of "man up". I didn't have a safe circle of friends where I was nurtured. I'm thankful I did have some friends, but they weren't educated about how it was okay for a man to display emotion and how the effects of holding them in could result in emotional leakage. During these walks, I started to rap over a beat. I enjoy poetry, as it's a way for me to express myself and talk about emotions, while also being a creative outlet.

Reflecting back on this dark season, I can see how far I've come. I'm now thankful to be on the other side, because it helped me grow as a person. As you can probably tell, during this time, I thought the world was against me. I felt sorry for myself and continued to delay putting my health first. I wasn't operating on a values system. I had what's called a victim mentality. As Jordan Peterson says in his book *12 Rules for Life*, "Treat yourself like someone you are responsible for helping".

CHAPTER 5: Emotions

I'm now armed with techniques that help me be more present and have a better vocabulary to define my emotions, as well as invest my time into like-minded individuals. Emotions are so important to learn about, and they're essential in knowing who you are. I will go into more detail in the next chapter about triggers, but know that in 2020, emotional intelligence (EQ) was one of the top ten skills needed to thrive/flourish. Another six of the top ten can be seen as subsections of EQ.

Emotion is energy in motion (e-motion). Einstein marvelled how our intuition is a beautiful gift, and our rational brain is a faithful servant. Jonice Webb, in her book *Running on Empty*, says, "Emotional neglect often sets us up for problems with self-indulgence". So we must be aware of this in order to label and adopt a *valiant mindset*.

According to Daniel Goleman in his book *Emotional Intelligence*, emotion is subjective, but you need to recognise that your emotional brain was formed through humanity's evolution. The first to take shape was the olfactory system (your sense of smell), and as it evolved, eventually formed the rational brain. Electrical signals pass through the limbic system, where your emotions and memories are, long before they get to where rational thinking takes place. Jonice explains that "Human emotions originate in the limbic system, which is buried deep below the cerebral cortex, the section of the brain where thought originates... They're physiological parts of our bodies, like fingernails or knees".

Therefore, all rational thoughts venture through the emotional part of your brain to get to the communication part, so you must own your emotions. However, know that through certain techniques, you can reframe your feelings and perception of them. Optimism is a choice. It can be learned and is the North Star to a higher state of being. You must honour your emotions and seek to understand and work with them to build a healthy adult. As you work on your emotions, you increase your flexion with your physiological parts and adapt to continue your deep connection with yourself.

The Three Areas of the Brain

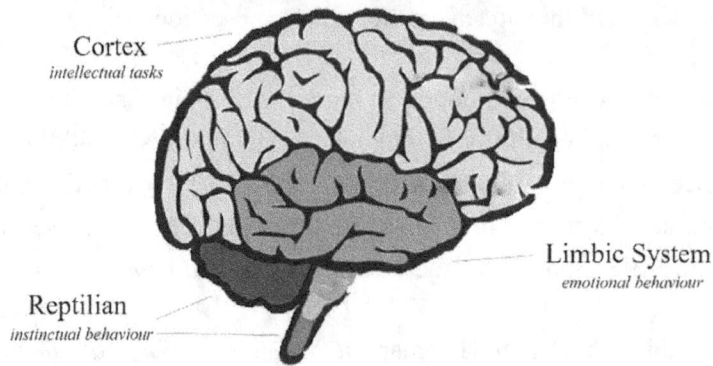

Cortex
intellectual tasks

Limbic System
emotional behaviour

Reptilian
instinctual behaviour

Emotional Reframing Techniques
1. Learn your emotional vocabulary
There's a helpful list at the back of this book.

2. Locate your emotion in your body
Label it, colour it, watch it transform and note the beauty.

3. Have gratitude
Having gratitude leads to more positive emotions, and you don't get sick as often.

Keep a gratitude journal. Each morning, write down three things you're grateful for, three things that would make your day great and an affirmation.

CHAPTER 5: Emotions

At night, write down three things that made your day, adding why it did, and finally, what you could have improved.

4. Have a positive emotion playlist on your phone/music streaming platform. This will trigger you to a more positive state.

5. Have a positive emotion photo
   This could be of a goal or family member.

6. Reframe the phrase "I have to", and change it to "I get to"
   It can be a game-changer.

7. Take cold showers
   It invigorates your extremities.

8. Go for a workout, or take a walk
   It releases feel-good brain chemicals.

CHAPTER 6
EMOTIONAL TRIGGERS

Most people use their energy attempting to rearrange circumstances that trigger painful emotions. Changing external circumstances will not change your rigid patterns of emotional response. That requires looking at the patterns themselves.

- Gary Zukav

CHAPTER 6: EMOTIONAL TRIGGERS

An emotional trigger is like a gun trigger. It propels you rapidly towards an emotion. According to Daniel Goleman, this is an *emotional hijacking*, which refers to a situation where the amygdala, the emotional-processing part of the brain, hijacks or bypasses the reasoning process. An emotional trigger can be positive or negative, such as seeing a newborn baby smiling or getting into a car crash.

After many years of reflection, healing, boundary-setting and self-compassion, I'm now at the point where I can vulnerably share my story.

At one time, I had a group of associates who would call me gay. When this happened, I'd suddenly feel as if they knew my past somehow, and a sense of shame would come over me. In his book *Emotional Intelligence 2.0*, David Bradberry sorted emotions into three categories in regard to intensity of feelings: low, medium and high. This wasn't a *low-intensity* emotion or normal sense of shame, such as feeling silly or guilty, but was a *high-intensity* emotion that gave me a sense of worthlessness, disgrace, dishonour and mortification. What my friends perceived as playful banter, took me back to a time when the younger version of myself was vulnerable and taken advantage of. This feeling froze the current version of me, and all senses were lost. I didn't have the tools to communicate, and this fuelled adversity.

Emotional triggers come from emotional stimuli. The longer the stories go, the stronger the emotion associated with it. At the time, I wasn't educated around triggers and awareness, which meant that I started to question my worth.

CHAPTER 6: Emotional Triggers

Triggers can make you feel helpless and that something bad will happen. The deeper the trigger, the less logical thinking occurs. When you take back the oppressive perception that you're a victim of your circumstances, you can grow into a healthy adult.

Physiologically, what happens is that your adrenaline tube gets filled up, and the body creates chemicals that turn into fight, flight or freeze. Here, the logic is gone, and physiologically, you get dumber the more emotional you get. The deeper and more intense the emotions grow, you enter emotional paralysis and wind up emotionally hijacked.

Essentially, everyone has two brains; the emotional and the rational. When you're coming from the emotional section, it can result in the rational brain not being present and operating. This is the effect gossiping has on people. If you ever see a person gossiping, look into their eyes. It's as if they're not present. This is the effect of the frontal lobe not being operational.

Awareness is the key. It is constant. Anticipate that emotional triggers may arise, but you need to relax and stay in the present, so your logical thinking can kick in. However, your efforts can be jeopardised by bad habits, the ego, associations, caving, boundaries, fear and pride. What do you think is jeopardising you? Feel free to use your pen and paper to write them down.

Now, you may think this doesn't apply to you, but I will ask you if you ever get frustrated, furious, enraged, hurt or dejected when your boss or partner says something that hits on a sensitive topic for you. This is called an *emotional trigger*. You can even trigger yourself. You know the feeling in your gut when you come across someone you don't want to see? That person can cause an emotional trigger. So now you know how to be aware, which is an essential part of understanding how to unhook and defuse from the trigger. In this case, it won't grow in momentum and cause high-intensity emotions. Instead, you'll merely be unhappy, moody, uptight, irritated or touchy, which are much easier to manage. Do you ever wonder why some people are cruel? When they call you names, are critical or just downright mean, this is a reflection of how they feel about themselves. Oftentimes, the dirt we see on other people is on the lens of our own glasses.

For me I felt isolated, I didn't know who I was, and repressed memories would trigger emotions in me that at the time, I couldn't label or manage. What ensued was an identity crisis.

Jim Qwik says, "Some of the most successful people live at the edge of their limits". I was brought up in a house with a mother who I remember as being in bed a fair amount of time, and a sister who stepped up with nurturing and caring for me. My mum and dad didn't get on, so my dad left when I was around eleven-years-old. He's a true champion who conquered cancer four times, and I'm forever grateful to him for teaching me patience and having a great work ethic. I mean, who sends their thirteen-year-old on a newspaper round, when the newspapers are bigger than he is? My dad used to drive me around on the weekends in his Porsche Boxster. Imagine looking out your window and seeing your newspaper being delivered by a kid in a Porsche! He'd beaten cancer that nearly took his life, so why not get a Porsche? But the fuel was more expensive than the ten pounds I was paid.

Being brought up in a house full of females, I'm grateful to have learned about how women work, what chivalry is and how to make women feel safe. However, I'm also a feminine male. I enjoy art due to my melancholy ways, and I'm often viewed as being in touch with

CHAPTER 6: Emotional Triggers

my feminine side. The Spanish half of my family are florists, so I love flowers, too. I believe this is the origin of what triggered me when I was called gay. As a side note, I would also like to share that I'm a recovering people pleaser/energy jeopardiser/caretaker, which I will go into more detail about below.

Let me take you back to my primary school days. My mum had a few jobs. She was a drugs sales rep, sold books and worked as a midwife. Due to my mum juggling responsibilities, I became independent at a young age, and would catch the school bus in the neighbouring part of the borough to West Wickham.

I was a young boy, my mind was evolving and I was learning who I was. I would try to fit in with other kids and always had a keen interest in other humans, as I was figuring out attachments. Why were their mum and dad together? Why was their house so different? These were the types of questions I would ask.

I'm giving you a trigger warning. This next piece of information is not enjoyable, but it's what happened in my life, and I believe it has sculpted me. As Adler says, "No matter what has occurred in your life up to this point, it should have no bearing at all on how you live from now on", so I believe in the mantra of not walking forward while looking back.

The reason I'm sharing this story is to help you understand that whatever you go through, it has no bearing on the person you will become. I'm now a lot more emotionally intelligent, so I'm able to tell my story without reservation and unhook from it.

Because there was no security at the school, I would go to other peoples' houses at the end of the day to wait for my mum to pick me up. There was one specific house I would go to, along with a friend of mine. An older boy lived there who would get us to partake in oral intimate acts that primary school kids should never do. This became a repressed trauma in my life, until I wound up being called gay by my friends.

These so-called mates at the time didn't understand what they were unsettling within me. I had feelings of shame, unworthiness and not being a good human. I was triggered into an extremely uncomfortable state, one of hyperarousal, which dysregulated my nervous system. It's the same biological state you go into when your life is being threatened.

When I was called gay, emotions would flood my amygdala gland, which is an almond-sized object at the back of the brain that secretes endorphins into the brain where the fight-or-flight syndrome is triggered. It resulted in hypervigilant activity, putting my whole body in a high state of stress. This was a huge adrenaline dump, where I would be overridden with the feeling you get when your life is threatened.

After years of working on myself, I've learned who my real friends are.

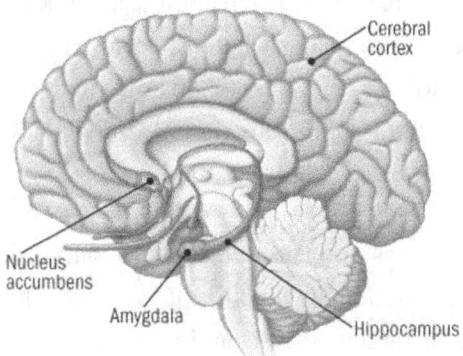

I had a fragile mindset back then and would jeopardise my own self to help others. I was a people-pleasing addict. A caretaker addict.

CHAPTER 6: Emotional Triggers

I had a strong Roman Catholic upbringing. On the weekends when I was with my dad, we went to church. Religion is forever changing, but at that time, homosexuality wasn't as accepted as it is now. I'm happy for the people who can be who they are and live their lives comfortably in their own skin. We're all perfect until anyone proves otherwise, so love your fellow humans, as we're all the same race and species.

I have learned techniques that I will now share with you about how to be present, have healthier boundaries, disassociate with the wording and be yourself. It has taken me a great amount of time and working with a specialist to heal and understand the past and send love to little Alex. I have learned through the technique of *diffusion* to get through this. It's what has given me a burning desire to write this book and share with others.

So, what were the steps to overcoming such a traumatic event? First, with the help of a specialist, I worked on what my masculine and feminine traits were, and then what boundaries and assertive language I could use, followed by more mindful techniques. I now meditate every morning, so I can connect/be in control of who I am and how my day will go. I also don't associate with people who don't have my best interests at heart. Just because we once had common interests, doesn't mean they should remain a permanent part of my life. Through my choices and understanding/awareness of certain traits, I was able to start the disassociation process with word and thought.

If you don't make your days count, then you will lose count of your days. Triggers come from your thoughts, so when you have a clearer head space, you will have fewer hijacking moments. I see this as mindfulness bandwidth. Mindfulness is kindness, which is not only how you treat others, but how you treat yourself. We're often so busy in society, that we forget to be kind to ourselves. In an aeroplane, when the mask falls, you must put yours on first. This is a life lesson. You help yourself before you can help others. Your thoughts have a direct correlation to the way you treat yourself.

Darren Hardy talks about the three ways to change your thoughts, and they are:

1. **Input**

    What are you listening to and watching? Are you entertaining your brain with murder documentaries, or are you conscientious like Oprah, as to what you allow in?

    I have a friend who loves watching murder documentaries and learning about the mind of a serial killer. Needless to say, when they're alone, where do you think their thoughts go?

    Due to their input, their reality is related to feeling and thinking that someone may kill them or suspecting other people to be murderers. Their obsession escalated when this person went on vacation and stayed in a rented house with some friends at a time when a certain documentary series was at its peak. My friend called to let me know that someone had been killed there. They were convinced there was blood everywhere, even though none was visible. Everybody was giddy, but I reassured them an AirBNB in Melbourne would not be a crime scene.

    Input affects perception.

CHAPTER 6: Emotional Triggers

2. **Association**

    Who do you invest your time into? Are they energy vampires, or do they bring you up?

    John Maxwell, a leadership expert, says that we are the sum of the top five people we associate with. As you can probably tell from my story about my associates, this wasn't a wholesome environment for me. Dave Ramsey says, "Who you surround yourself with will determine the height you are able to climb".

3. **Environment**

    Environment dictates performance.

    If you wanted to get good at basketball, would you start playing with a group of beginners or pros? Personally, I'd want to be with the pros, even though it would be the most uncomfortable, because the reward would be far greater and offer the most growth.

My mentor taught me that "The solution to pollution is dilution", and he was so right! By taking into consideration your input, association and environment, you're making the pollution in your life heavier and denser, or clearer and transparent. As you can see in the diagram below, males and females grow and change throughout the different stages of life. Have you ever looked back at your life and loved that younger version of yourself? Do you have empathy for their struggles and take the time to rewire any hooked memories?

This diagram shows how the body ages and the stages of our growth and development. You are forever evolving/adapting/changing.

Sigmund Freud was a pioneer of theories behind how we're connected to our mind, body and spirit. He said that everything we do springs from two motives: sexual urges and the desire to be great. I'd like to break down the desire to be great. John Dewey understood this as the need to be important. We can further break down this idea into three strands:

- The desire to be seen.

- The desire to be heard.

- The desire to fit in.

Every human on this planet wants to be seen and heard. We also want to fit in, as we're social beings. All of this can be proven by the popularity of social media and the need for "likes". We're not isolated snow leopards or tigers of the Bangladesh deltas, but a species that gathers around fire pits to share stories.

In 1953, Dr Seuss showed us how important it is for us humans to fit in. His book, *The Sneetches*, follows the story of yellow bird-like creatures called Sneetches. Some of them have green stars on their bellies, and some do not. The ones without a star want to fit in, so they meet with an entrepreneur, Sylvester McMonkey McBean, who has a machine to put a star on their belly.

But while the non-star-bellied Sneetches pay to use the machine, the ones with the star want to remain unique, so they meet with Sylvester to reverse it. By the end, all of the Sneetches have lost their money. It's

CHAPTER 6: Emotional Triggers

supposed to be a metaphor for how people will give up everything they have in order to fit in and feel special. Does this sound similar to our current society, with people getting tattoos and filling their face with toxins? Another philosophical point Dr Seuss wanted to make was a saying made famous by Bernard Baruch, that goes, "Those who mind don't matter, and those who matter don't mind". I will talk more about this in the next chapter.

There are three stages to human growth:

1. Dependence
   We are born dependent on our parent who take care of all our needs.

2. Independence
   We go out into the world and take care of ourselves.

3. Interdependence
   Though some do slip back to being dependant and either never move out or come back home, it's usually the third stage of being a healthy adult where we become interdependent, which means being willing to become vulnerable to another person in order to create emotional intimacy.

I'm now at a level of emotional intelligence where I've reached interdependence and am comfortable being vulnerable enough to talk about triggers, which can be all-encompassing and detrimental to living a contented life. Mental health is becoming a more open subject without negative connotation. My perception is that it's the gym for the mind. As a physically obese person abuses their body, so does a mentally ill person. But the difference is that since the damage takes place internally, you can't see it, and you might not take it as seriously. Being aware of emotional triggers is a game-changer, as it arms you with the ability to separate the emotion from what's actually happening.

It's the inner dialogue that will help you on your emotional growth journey, where you're able to send self-compassion and identify that it's a thought, so you can remain present and know you're safe. You're the master of your fate, steering your own ship to success. The more you improve your self-management, the more your healthy adult grows, because you start to recognise emotions as indicators, not dictators. Your emotions inform you; they don't control you. When you have awareness of what your emotional triggers are, you can highlight them, move through them and grow.

Shifting from emotions to awareness is different than being caught up in them. You're able to be present. This will arm you to live a fulfilled life. You can now be an observer. It's like being at a busy train station and being able to choose the train, the track and the destination, rather than only having access to one track line. Awareness is constant.

Grounding Tools

Grounding exercises are the key to staying in the present. The following questions are the ones I used when I was overcome with a high sense of emotion due to memories being triggered. Grounding is essential in not only hypervigilant times, but also day to day.

> **Sensory Techniques, the FSSH principle:**

   ✓ What are you Feeling?

   ✓ What are you Seeing?

CHAPTER 6: Emotional Triggers

- ✓ What are you Smelling?

- ✓ What are you Hearing?

If you find yourself being hooked to a trigger, like a fssh is hooked on a fishing line, this is the fssh principle you should use. Count ten things you can feel/touch/taste, see, smell, and hear. This technique should bring you back to being present and in control of your body.

> **Situational Questions/Techniques:**

- ✓ What just happened?

- ✓ What are these feelings telling me?

- ✓ Write it down. (Allow yourself to understand your feelings about what happened)

Diffusion Tools

As a fish latches onto a hook, so can your thoughts. In order to unhook from them, you can use certain techniques. Speaking out loud is helpful in severely traumatic experiences, such as a car crash. Talking about it while you're in the situation will help you rationalise what's going on.

There are many ways to tell if your thoughts are in charge and running your old operating system. The Thanking Approach is one I find particularly helpful.

> **The Thanking Approach**

  ✓ Say out loud, "Thank you for that thought. I'm not going to listen to it". And then carry on.

  ✓ Use your silly voice to vocalise your thoughts. You could do a Mickey/Minnie Mouse impression, repeating the word, or something really high-pitched.

This technique will unhook you from traumatic memories or any activity that arouses hyperactivity, while also increasing the Losada ratio.

Thought Tools
The leaves on a stream technique gives you an underlying premise of what thoughts are. There are also other analogies, such as sitting at the side of a busy freeway and watching cars going past that may help, but in essence, a thought is something that comes and goes. What matters is your decision to listen to it or not.

> **Leaves on a stream**

  Imagine a beautiful, calm stream surrounded by lovely moss-covered trees. As you look to the left, you notice a leaf start flowing down the stream.

  You watch the leaf as it bounces off the side of the stream and then spins like a ballerina, pirouetting, before it bumps into a rock. Just as it's about to drift on, the stream's current keeps it there for a little while.

CHAPTER 6: Emotional Triggers

Then the leaf turns and continues down the stream, dunking in the water, spinning around, only to encounter another rock. The leaf is stuck again, the top part flapping in the oncoming water, as yet again it pirouettes and continues down the stream.

You watch the leaf as it glides out of vision before again refocusing your attention on the stream and the beautiful surroundings, as you feel the warm sun on your cheeks.

You look to your left and see that another leaf has entered the stream, dancing and spinning, before it again crashes into a rock.

The leaf being stuck on the rock is a symbol of how much power and attention you give your thoughts. Every day, your mind will have thoughts that you can't control when they arise. You can influence them through input, association and environment, but you won't be able to control them if you empower them.

Here are some ways you can direct how your thought pattern goes.

- ✓ When having negative thoughts, ask yourself, *Would I speak to someone else like this?* Most of the time, you wouldn't, so why would you speak to yourself this way? This technique is useful when in embarrassing or shameful situations.

- ✓ Increasing your emotional vocabulary means that you're able to define it and either increase the good feeling or take away the power of unpleasant feelings. For instance, take the word "happy". What you need to ask yourself instead is if you're feeling joyful, enthralled, ecstatic, playful. Or consider the word "anger". It's better to ask if you're feeling frustrated, sad, depressed or enraged.

- ✓ Know you have a choice regarding the stories you tell yourself and whether to wallow in the emotion or live your life and take your power back from these triggers. The more power you give them, the more the rational side of your brain switches off, so you need to dilute them.

Knowing you're human and imperfect is what makes you perfect.

CHAPTER 7
EMOTIONAL WAVE

*You can't stop the waves,
but you can learn how to surf.*

- Swami Satchidananda

CHAPTER 7: EMOTIONAL WAVE

Emotional wave is a term that was introduced to me by my EQ mentor. While a tide is slow and creeps in, a wave can also be something that comes in fast. An example would be a tsunami which is a wave and different from a trigger, however, with a tsunami the water remains long after it's over. A trigger is there and gone.

An emotional wave is unpredictable. You can't foresee what's coming, but when you're triggered, sometimes that wave hits you in the back when you least expect it. Using the grounding techniques I've already taught, you can ride that wave in.

While reopening my now vintage iPhone 5s, I saw photos from the past three years, which put me about halfway through my seven-year skin-shedding cycle and took me into an emotional wave where I wasn't fully present. But I was fortunate enough to have the techniques that helped me acknowledge this time and just go on with my journey. I knew I was okay and that I owned my thoughts, but I wasn't fully aware at the time about the wave.

In life, you have to go through the valleys to get to the peaks, but you first need to acknowledge them. When you're in the valley, this is where character is built. The next peak will be even bigger than the last, and that's the beauty of weathering the storm. You have to be self-compassionate during these times, as you're susceptible to being self-critical, which won't help you become a healthy adult.

CHAPTER 7: Emotional Wave

Life Principle

A great life principle to follow is Michael Phelps. This man is a champion who's won twenty-three gold medals and is known for his heart connection to the water. From 2014-2017, he set world records for many types of swimming competitions. What did he do to get there? He trained hard. Michael perfected and optimised his aerodynamics by not turning his head. He simply didn't have the *time* to see what was going on in other lanes, because it would only breed comparison. *Michael Phelps stayed in his own lane.*

At the end of the day, life is like a game of chess; strategic, beautiful and wonderous if you move forwards. But the enemy you're playing against is time, so when you don't make a move, it has a counter-move.

Michael stays on his own path. He can't expend his effort, energy and power looking in other lanes. In which parts of your life do you need to stay in your own lane?

There's a realisation that you're removing emotional bandwidth from others, as you're taken up by the emotional wave, which results in not being present for them. This is good to remember, so you can be quick to recognise when you're on a wave and alert others. Let them know you're okay and working on some emotional stuff that has nothing to do with them. Of course, this assumes you're with your inner circle of most-trusted people. Communication is essential. Something I like to say is, "Hey, my being is working on something at the moment, and I'm on an emotional wave, so I wanted to give you a heads up". Communication is key, and the people who matter won't mind.

One day I was talking to my friend Braden about the moon and how different phases can have a distinct effect on you. The human adult body is made of sixty percent water, while the brain and heart are composed of seventy-three percent, and the lungs eighty-three percent. This means that in much the same way the moon affects the tides, it's obvious we must also be affected.

Braden reported how he was managing to progress through this time, whereas I was surfing an emotional wave. But I was staying the course, submitting and going with it.

Addressing and being aware of the wave is the first step of conscious learning. But understanding what change is needed is only the beginning. In order to actually implement this knowledge, here are the four stages of learning, as coined by psychologists.

Stages of Learning

1. Unconscious Incompetence
   You don't know that you don't know.

2. Conscious Incompetence
   You know that you don't know.

3. Conscious Competence
   You know that you know.

4. Unconscious Competence
   You don't know that you know.

Basically, the first stage is that you're unaware of the skill and how to do it. The second is becoming aware of the skill, but you can't do it. The third is utilising the skill with effort, and the fourth is when it becomes an unconscious habit, like tying your shoes.

❯ Grounding Techniques

- ▶ Dropping the anchor
  Ideally, you should do this when you're not on a wave.
  Practice putting your fingertips together and closing your eyes while imagining you've dropped an anchor within your body. Sit with your being for a few minutes, and then open your eyes.

- ▶ Regulating your breath
  This will help you become present in your current being. An easy, go-to technique, is where you breathe in for a count of five, and out for five. Repeat this ten times.

- ▶ Changing the temperatures in the shower
  Put it on cold. It often helps but is hard to execute.

- ▶ Communication
  Verbalise what's going on.

- ▶ Self-Compassion
  Be compassionate to yourself

- ▶ Be adaptable
  Don't hold on to your values so tightly.

- ▶ Know this will pass
  Acknowledge that it's only a feeling, and it will go away.

CHAPTER 8
THE 4 A'S

Ability is what you're capable of doing. Motivation determines what you do. Attitude determines how well you do it.

- Lou Holtz

CHAPTER 8: THE 4 A'S

In an effort to teach you how to regulate your emotions and thoughts, I would like to introduce you to the 4 A's, which are essential in building, knowing and living your identity. I live these every day. They are virtues that through compassion and empathy, are mood elevators, where you choose which floor you go to. You will never outgrow your expectations. These four awareness symbols help you choose how high up you go. You have choices in life. Your introspective decisions are challenging, and that is what makes the reward so fulfilling. It's through growth goals that you receive such magic.

Authenticity

> *Living excellently doesn't mean simply being efficient, it means living with superhigh integrity, with loyalty, and with commitment to a value system as a solid foundation.*
>
> - Dave Ramsey

How do you even know your level of authenticity or self-awareness? How does authenticity impact your performance? Have you noticed that being inauthentic leads to disappointment?

Authenticity is being who you are. If you're on a road to self-discovery, then I highly recommend writing your values down and keeping them visible.

CHAPTER 8: The 4 A's

Did you know that, according to Nielsen ratings, the average Australian spends an average of two and a half hours a day watching live TV and recorded content? On a monthly basis, this equates to almost seventy-five hours! Imagine if you turned this time into something that would benefit your future.

The term "busy" frustrates me, as it's often worn as a badge of honour. What this actually means is that you haven't efficiently prioritised your time. Being busy is not being authentic to yourself. If you're constantly saying you don't have time to get everything done, look at your television-viewing habits. Each human has the same twenty-four hours in the day to be their authentic self, just like Elon Musk does, and how Einstein and Michelangelo once did. The difference-maker is distractions.

If you've written down your values, congratulations on taking the first step. Most people don't get this far!

The second step is to live by your values, which will become a dominating thought over time, as it contributes to your authenticity. I'm not saying that anybody is perfect, and I'm not, either. As Deepak Chopra says, "We are spiritual beings who have taken physical form to fulfil a purpose". Perfection is a harsh word that applies too much pressure and should be taken out of people's vocabularies. My motto is, *Chase progress, not perfection.*

Of course, the opposite is also true, and eliminating all competition and a need to strive for a goal, could lead to complacency.

An example of value-living is maintaining good health. My morning routine solidifies this value, where I eat clean, stretch, do yoga and then journal and concentrate on learning new things (health for the mind).

Let's speak theoretically here. I've just gifted you a Lamborghini, and you're driving it around town, enjoying showing it off, when you realise it's low on fuel. What would you do? Naturally, you'd want to fuel up your new beauty, so you go to a petrol station. Now you have a choice to make. Do you get the cheapest fuel, the mid-range or the highest premium quality?

Your body is the most complex engine in the world. In your first stage of life, you were dependant. You didn't need to stress about what fuel was going into it. But as you grew up, you might not have made the best choices. As Jim Qwik says, "If an egg is broken by an outside force, life ends. If an egg is broken by an inside force, life begins". So, what are you going to change to live authentically and be your whole self? You are a compilation of subconscious habits, and most of the time you don't even realise what you're putting into your system. Again, in no way am I perfect. Heck, I enjoy fried chicken with my friends on the weekend from time to time. Perfection is not what this is about.

This process does take *time*, *patience* and *persistence*, but it's worth it. I'd like to put the emphasis on patience, as success is the compilation of small, seemingly insignificant habits or rituals done daily that lead to radical results. Patience is the fruit of your trials. It's delaying the gratification. Patience is strength of character, which gives you the ability to endure.

A subsection of authenticity is integrity, which is living by your values. And according to John Maxwell, author of *Developing the Leader Within You*, "Integrity is the human quality most necessary to business success". Having a solid reputation, not only with others but with yourself, causes increased self-esteem. Have you realised how integrity has the word *grit* in the middle of it?

In order to be authentic, you need to connect with your heart and with

CHAPTER 8: The 4 A's

others. My mentor, Lisa Lyons, taught me that, "Hustle and heart will set you apart". Leading your life with heart will cause many doors to open, thus increasing your results. Your heart is your energy centre. It literally sends a pulse around your body.

If you agree that character-building is following through on actions long after the emotion has gone, then you can understand there are consequences for inaction and the excuses that go with it. This self-deception accompanies an old Spanish proverb: *he who does not look ahead, remains behind.*

These are the five stages of self-deception:

> **Stage One: Acting on your current emotion**
> Have you ever vowed to go to the gym or sort out the cupboards, but then don't immediately take action? You promise yourself you'll get on it first thing tomorrow, but when the next day comes, you decide you're too busy, so you put it off until tomorrow, and so on. I call this "acting on your current emotion", which isn't good for your self-confidence or authenticity. Here's a reality check: when you haven't committed to living your authentic self, tomorrow never comes. It's the first stage of self-deception and a deterrent of authenticity.
> *I can't be bothered.*

> **Stage Two: Justifying your betrayal**
> Seeing the world in a way that justifies your self-betrayal. You decide that you don't need to take these actions, because they're unimportant and unnecessary. And if you come to believe this idea fully, you'll feel you've "won" this battle with your mind, and therefore don't have to follow through on any positive actions.
> *It's fine.*

> **Stage Three: Seeing the world through a distorted lens**
> You pursue self-deception. Your perception of reality is now slightly distorted. You've convinced yourself you don't need to take action.
> *It doesn't matter anyway.*

> **Stage Four: Identifying with your self-deception**
> You're now characterised by this deception. It's part of who you feel you are.
> *That's not me.*

> **Stage Five: Carrying the self-deception**
> Your betrayal and self-deception have become characteristics you carry with you. This is now who you are. You are vibrating at a lower level than your potential.
> *I don't do that.*

Al Capone rose to be a mobster boss, running businesses that were not in line with the law. How do you think he felt about his actions? Do you believe he saw himself as the lawbreaker he was? No. He had an image of himself as hard-working and deserving of all the money, fame and glory he received, which only entrenched him deeper into his criminal behaviour and made him bolder.

The more immersed in the process you become, the more you move away from being in line with your values.

CHAPTER 8: The 4 A's

5 steps of self-deception

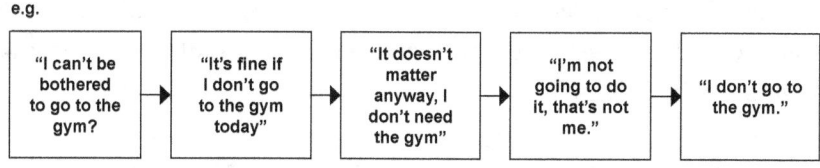

You can see how this downward spiral can harvest a lack of authenticity of your character. It's time to decide who you want to be. I know when I was overweight, I wasn't as happy, confident and flourishing as I am now. I'm not saying I'm at my peak yet, but I try very hard to stay healthy in order to be authentic to my soul.

I feel that elements of charisma are part of authenticity. John Maxwell, in his book, *Everyone Communicates, Few Connect*, says that anyone can be charismatic. "You just need to be positive, believe in yourself, and focus on others". I know it may be easier said than done, but being optimistic and positive is a choice.

There are only ever two cups you can fill at any given time. In this case, it's authentic and inauthentic. It may take a while to figure out who you are if your vision is polluted, but you'll get there. I used to be consumed by darkness. Since then, I've worked hard to switch this around, and do you know what? Life is a lot better. I enjoy cheering others up, like the man in the butcher shop or the elderly lady down the street. Do you know why people wear certain clothes, jewellery or watches? It's to impress others. Feel free to be genuine, and compliment someone or ask them how their day is going. Just being the light for somebody is charismatic in its own way.

Coach Wooden, one of basketballs greatest coaches, used to live by a principle of "Be true to yourself". He would even print it out, laminate it and give it to people such as Lew Acindor, who was subjected to a racial slur. He said he never forgot this advice and went on to score record-setting numbers throughout his career.

People pleasers, you know when you're not being true to yourself when your gut says *no*, and you say *yes*. Always follow through on your word. It's your bond and proof that you're living authentically.

As Hamlet proclaims:

This above all: to thine own self be true,

And it must follow, as the night the day,

Thou canst not then be false to any man."

Techniques for Achieving Authenticity

⟩ **Sit with yourself**

I recommend meditation. You're the person to worship, the one to make sacrifices for and be humble towards.

⟩ **Be genuine**

Have integrity. Say what you mean, and mean what you say. Follow through on your words with action, and don't make a commitment you know you can't fulfil, because you're not doing anyone any favours.

CHAPTER 8: The 4 A's

> **Have Self-Assurance**

Confidence is built through repetition of courageous acts, which leads to knowing who you are.

> **Embody the principle of today, not tomorrow (TNT)**

Tomorrow never comes when you're not committed.

> **Practice creative hopelessness**

This is an acceptance and commitment therapy (ACT) tool that helps patients reassess their goals and values. They identify how they've been avoiding their pain, and then evaluate through their lived experience what that avoidance has cost them.

Patients then have an opportunity to explore a new pathway of living fuller lives *with* their pain. They can imagine what their lives would be like if they tried accepting what they can't control and shifting behaviours around what they can.

> **Love your inner child**

You should love your inner child. If you never think of them, go to a mirror, look at yourself and say, "I love you", and you will see the inner child. Do it. You'll thank me.

Connect to this younger, smaller version of yourself. A great way to heal memories is to go back as your current self and hold hands with your younger version to re-write the memory. If this is too much to do on your own, seek professional assistance.

Be objective and truthful as you answer these questions.

Questions to help you reflect on your Authenticity

✓ What are some of the decisions you've made?

✓ Why did you make those decisions?

✓ Its easier to decide which of the decisions are authentic if you have identified them first.

✓ Did you truly have the freedom to make those decisions, or did someone else persuade you to make them?

✓ Were your reasons authentic, or did people-pleasing drive you to make them?

✓ What values drove your decisions?

✓ Did the outcomes and the manner you achieved them accurately reflect your core true values? Would those closest to you agree?

✓ What do your decisions reveal about you? Your motives? Your values?

✓ Is there any underpinning pain or hurt that may be causing or driving your decisions?

Introspection is reflection to renew your mind. This journey is a process, not an event. If your actions come from a dishonest place, you will hurt people, but if you're being authentic and true to yourself, you can heal yourself and others.

CHAPTER 8: The 4 A's

Accountability

> *Time flies, but you are the pilot. You are the master of your fate and captain of your soul.*
>
> - Anonymous

Where you are currently in your life is the result of how you think. Placing blame signifies a victim mentality and gets you nowhere. Trust me. I've been there. You can blame as much as you want, but it won't help you progress.

As I've previously spoken about, you were not put on this planet to just live a mundane life but to have purpose. Extreme ownership comes into play, as you have complete control over your destiny. However, if you fall into a despair cycle or get entrenched in your thoughts, it can be detrimental for you.

A lot of people aren't taught this principle, Parents feel that they are "doing this to help you". They feel they're acting in good faith, as they don't want you making the same mistakes they have. Parents with a guilty conscience can cause a lot of problems for the child. Though their motives may be pure, they could be doing irreparable damage. Your issue is your life, so your accountability should be what you reflect upon.

The best investment you can make is in yourself. This is known as *personal equity*. Nowadays, we're information rich and discernment poor, and have a hard time telling the difference between fact and fiction. The internet, albeit useful, requires no accountability. You should research where the information comes from. Social media is a billboard

CHAPTER 8: The 4 A's

for opinions. These days, people often take what they've read as the truth and will repeat it without question.

Accountability is a difference-maker for yourself and others. You can't make excuses if you want to succeed. A mentor once taught me that making a decision equals murdering your options. Due to fear, and the human law of least effort, we like to give ourselves options. You must alleviate them and go for it, in order to achieve your goal.

If you're on a train, you know that it will make many stops before it gets to its destination. In life, there are many stops and starts. Be patient.

However, if you don't know the destination, then nobody does. Determination is the vehicle, and enthusiasm is the driver. Winston Churchill, who won a Nobel Prize in Literature (1953), remarked how success is going from failure to failure, without loss of enthusiasm. This was a man who made a historical impact on the human race.

Following through with what you say harvests accountability, and when you help yourself by figuring out your issues, it increases your self-equity, and you become a leader. A manager is somebody who tells people what to do, but a leader embodies what's needed. Once you master becoming a leader, you make an impact.

Your self-esteem is the covenant you make with yourself, but if you've gone through the self-deception phases, then your subjective view may be distorted. The ultimate goal is for your thoughts to match your words and actions. Thoughts are magical things that are the by-product of your past. They are not you. It's your choice to give these thoughts power. As Les Giblin says in *How to Have Confidence and Power in Dealing with People*, "Low self-esteem means friction and trouble," If the other person has low self-esteem, they will project their pain onto others".

In order to deal with such frictional people, it's your role to lift them up. Then they can feel better about themselves, while you maintain your confidence, because you haven't allowed them to have an effect on your self-esteem.

Comparison can stint accountability and is the thief of joy, so you must become a first-rate you and not a second-rate somebody else. A huge part of accountability is the aspect of growth through accountability. A mistake is a *miss-take*, so look at it as a learning experience. However, repeating the same mistake and expecting a different outcome is the definition of insanity. So, in your search for wisdom, if you make a mistake, move on and try a different way. Don't be afraid of slipping up again and again, before you move forward. If you've never done something before, you won't be an expert at it on the first try. Remember that the word *success* starts with *suc*, so don't be afraid to "suck" at first. The great Olympian, Elka Whalen, once taught me that you're a student of life and not just an attendee. When you realise that *status* is **S**till **T**oo **A**rrogant **T**o **U**nderstand **S**uccess, then you're ready to move on. Elka was blessed to be taught how her subconscious could steer her life by her father, who poured positive affirmations into her as she drifted off to sleep.

Your subconscious never turns off, and you can supercharge it by telling it what to work on, even as you sleep. Napoleon Hill teaches about the concept of auto-suggestion, where you talk directly to your subconscious, in his book *Think and Grow Rich*, which is a term coined by French psychologist Emil Coué.

CHAPTER 8: The 4 A's

Change is inevitable, and growth is optional. The only thing that may not give you change is a vending machine! Unfortunately, you're conditioned from a young age that growth is a process. As a baby, you were completely dependent. Then you go to school, and by the time you come out, you're supposed to be independent. Your brain can be conditioned to have the perception that growth is a process, an infinite game mindset, and not a destination.

You mature by conquering challenges, which means you're either living in the stress zone or the stretch zone. The stretch zone is where you want to be, and you accomplish this by making small steps out of your comfort zone, until you accomplish your goal.

If you have a fantasy about how you want your life to be, write it down. It will give you clarity. Then break down your plan into smaller tasks, and give yourself goals as to when you want to achieve them. This will give you accountability and intensify your vision.

Patience is the power, and at its core is intensity, hope, vision and diligence.

As Dave Ramsey says, "It is human nature to want it and want it now; it is also a sign of immaturity. Being willing to delay pleasure for a greater result is a sign of maturity". Contentment is the destination and also the conduit. But none of it will mean anything if you don't follow through and become accountable, which means being true to yourself.

Techniques for Better Accountability

- **Zeigarnik Effect for Procrastination**.
  Break up your vision into bite-sized goals and time frames.

- **Pomodoro technique**
  Set a twenty-five-minute timer and then take a five-minute break. This is effective for accomplishing crucial tasks, and you can stack them on top of one another.

- **Repeat a mantra**
  "I know I have the ability to achieve my dream. Therefore, I demand of myself consistent and persistent action until it's achieved".

- **Keep a progress journal**

- **Have accountability or peak performance partners**

Adversity

Great suffering builds up a human being and puts him within the reach of self-knowledge.
-Anwar el-Sadat

Going through adversity is where you find the real you. I would never wish hardship upon anyone, but often it's needed to harden up and realise some of your problems aren't that bad in comparison. For instance, you may have trouble processing your emotions or are upset about not being able to go on vacation. But those who've suffered through real problems are families in slums and refugee camps, and those who worry about where their next meal is coming from.

CHAPTER 8: The 4 A's

Dale Carnegie says, "If you tell me how you get your feeling of importance, I'll tell you what you are. That determines your character. That is the most significant thing about you". What he means is that your need to be important can result in either positive or negative actions. For instance, a need for importance caused an impoverished Lincoln to read law books, while Dillinger's motivation was to be a criminal. Carnegie also says, "...and the rare individual who honestly satisfies this heart hunger will hold people in the palm of his or her hand". If you authentically know who you are, you can sit with yourself and genuinely add value to others to help them flourish.

When I had my scooter accident in 2016, I lost my love for my fellow humans. My schemas of mistrust were triggered, and my heart was hurting, therefore I didn't take my eyes off my problems. But after being in isolation for long periods of time, I figured out that by helping others, I would be helping myself. I'm now thankful this event occurred. At the time, while I was crying and not understanding why it happened, I thought it had broken me. Instead, it wound up raising the floor. I was able to play at a new level. It gave me the seed of introspection and connection with my authentic self.

Napoleon Hill says, "Every adversity, every failure, every heartbreak, carries with it the seed of an equal or greater benefit". This is where you can bring in your growth mindset to figure out what seeds you're nurturing. Life isn't all sunshine and rainbows. There will be challenges along the way.

I believe adversity is one of the most powerful tools that will help you rise above your current circumstances. Do you perceive yourself as a greatness accelerator? When you join the marines, you're sent to camps where they try to break you. By getting pushed to the edge, you will know within yourself what you can conquer. I see this as *the rubber band effect*. The more you're stretched beyond your bounds, the harder you will snap back.

Growing through adversity is the key to your own success. It's a bridge, not a wall. You can build walls when you concentrate on your own state of being, but when you build a bridge with optimism, it leads you to the next stage.

You have to identify whether you're going through a peak or a valley. Adversity will test you during your valley, but getting through it and coming out the other side will elevate you. This is where you must have humility. Be kind-natured and able to forward think when you're in the valley, knowing you will get to the next peak.

Life pushes you around, but you learn to move on. This is where you must live above the line. Emotions come into play, as well as learning how to defuse them. Adversity can flow into your life like a tidal wave, and you need to figure out how to persevere through it.

Failure is merely a wrong turn on the way to success. If you quit, then it was all a waste of time. This is where your growth mindset kicks in.

Frank Shamrock was a UFC champion who had a unity mindset that was similar to Bruce Lee's. He survived a lot of adversity in his life and had run-ins with the law, so he took what he learned growing up and came up with the Plus, Minus, Equals mindset.

CHAPTER 8: The 4 A's

Your plus is your mentor. A person who's gone through it, and who drives and aspires you to outperform them.

Each time you train with your minus, you would still be learning. It gives you humility to hone your skills.

Your equal is your competition, someone who gets the competitive drive growing in you.

As you can see, training with a mentor (your plus) enriches you and gets you to aim higher. The key is association and immersion. Who are you hanging out with? As they say, you are the sum total of the top five people with whom you surround yourself.

Your minus, someone who doesn't know as much as you do, can also be a valuable teacher. You gain humility and are able to hone your skills.

Here, your two cups are *resentment* and *forgiveness*. If you give into your need for revenge, it's like filling your resentment cup with poison and expecting the other person to be harmed. This is not reality. I spent my time after the bike accident stewing and scheming in my mind, and it just delayed my ascent. I didn't understand reactions in my body. I would cry every day on the way to work, not understanding that I was filling my resentment cup.

When you feed the negativity, you can't live your life in harmony. Having malice toward people, places and things, and having a good life, can't be present at the same time. Making money and making excuses can't be present at the same time. If you always think the way you've always thought, you will always get what you've always got.

Time is the most precious commodity, and in your job, you trade time for money. You might not recognise that you're going through adversity, because you've lost perspective. But if you have a mentor, somebody who can look at your situation objectively, they can offer you perspective.

With the knowledge that time is such a finite resource, what more could you achieve in your life? What can you start immediately and attach onto as you sacrifice another part of your life? Personal development comes at a cost. As you grow through the changes you make, you will attract different types of people and energies.

Immersion is the application of knowledge, which leads to wisdom. Adversity is where you identify resilience. You understand that you're maturing, and what you perceive as a big deal is thwarted. The understanding of adversity is empowering. It's identifying and is the unity of your being.

I would love to propose the story of The Wounded Soldier. The first Australian to receive the Victorian cross for his action in Gallipoli in 1915 was a legend named Albert Jacka. He was a great man who leapt into a trench, single-handedly killed seven Turkish soldiers and held the trench alone for the remainder of the night.

Within a year, Jacka was back on duty, when he was captured by German stormtroopers, along with forty-one others. During this time, Jacka was shot seven times. Two were in the head. Wounded, and with no weapons, he took on the might of the German captors with his bare hands, killing twelve soldiers and overthrowing the Germans.

But Jacka didn't stop there. In 1918, he was shot through the throat, and by the time he got out of hospital, the war was over. Upon returning

CHAPTER 8: The 4 A's

to Australia in 1929 he was elected mayor of St Kilda City Council in Melbourne, where he worked for the cause of unemployment with devotion and commitment.

Jacka died two years later, but not before leaving an impact on the world. He acted with honour, integrity and heart, someone who bounced back from adversity.

A wounded soldier is subjected to tests and battle scars, but they're all added to chinks in their armour. You will experience real adversity in your life, from family passing, to sicknesses and emotional upheavals. It's how you go from being wounded to overcoming it and fighting on, that is the core to your own success. You all have Jacka mentality in you.

There are three paths you can take with adversity.

- ✓ Let it destroy you

- ✓ Let it define you

- ✓ Let it strengthen you

The beauty of it is that it's really your choice. You're powerful beyond measure, and when you hit rock bottom, it can be a great foundation from which to grow.

People are attracted to value, and this is why you need to experience adversity to really appreciate your newfound life perspective. When you're low and going through that emotional wave, you need to know it's okay and to write your story in order to heal. Experiencing adversity is an opportunity for self-discovery and a catalyst for learning.

Resistance to the limitations that others may have, enables you to thrive.

Know that adversity causes pain and therefore is a catalyst for change. You don't get to choose what kind of adversity comes into your life, but you can choose your response to it.

Adversity has introduced me to myself. It's plumbed the depths of my heart. It's tested my strengths and highlighted my victim mentality, but also gave birth to my valiance.

Through introspection, awareness of the self is born. The realisation that life happens through you, not to you, is the weapon that slices through the **adversity**.

Breaking the word down, you have:

1. ad (addition)

2. verse (a Latin term meaning "to turn" or "to challenge". You can see this as a verse of a song also)

3. ity (a suffix used to form abstract nouns expressing a state or condition.)

So when broken down, ad-vers-ity is actually an addition to your story, dependent upon abstract expression.

In terms of adversity, your two cups are *fade* and *flourish*. If your response to adversity is to fill your fading cup, then the outcome will be negativity. But if you choose to fill your flourishing cup with the lessons you've learned, then you will see and experience the world in a different way, and situations will turn out in your favour.

CHAPTER 8: The 4 A's

> *Circumstances are but the rulers of the weak; they are but the instruments of the wise.*
> -Samuel Lover

There's a story of two Italian men who were friends from a young age. As children, they each decided to plant a mandarin tree. Both of the friends planted their tree and were having no luck. The first man gave it no real love. The second moved it and led it to a healthy root system, where years later this mandarin tree flourished.

This is an analogy for life. If you're in a place where you're not thriving and getting what you need, try removing yourself from your current situation and into a new one, or changing your perspective, and you will flourish beyond your wildest dreams.

> *Turn your wounds into wisdom.*
> -Oprah Winfrey

You're taught at school that mistakes are bad. That an F means failure. My view is that every miss-take is an opportunity.

We're currently in the middle of the Covid-19 pandemic and an economic recession, which will happen again in another decade or so. In the last recession of 2008-2010, Uber, Airbnb, Slack, WhatsApp and Square were all created. During every time of adversity there lies a seed. Wherever there's a low, there's a high. During world wars, where many people were killed, those who sold arms flourished. In this Covid chapter, people selling cleaning products are flourishing. It's all about perception.

Other companies and innovations that were born during a recession:

- ✓ Boeing 707 airliner: 1957
- ✓ Federal Express: 1973
- ✓ Apple iPod: 2001

Being static isn't an option in life, as time is always moving forward. Time is so precious, as once it's gone, it has forever disappeared. We as humans are continually adapting.

Some people treat adversity as a tombstone, others as a steppingstone. Which one would you choose?

Techniques for Tackling Adversity

> Plan for it

> One of my dear friends, James Rogers, used this technique to deal with the passing of his father. He managed his expectations as his father's health deteriorated, and though it was obviously difficult, his attitude helped him flourish.

> This is down to perception. MMA fighters know they will be challenged physically, so they spar and practice, which means by the time they get into the ring, they're in peak mental and physical condition. Adopting a champion mindset is the key to having power.

Techniques for Tackling Adversity and maintaining a Healthy Attitude during times of Adversity.

> Don't underestimate the problem.

> Living your value system helps you heal. The bigger the person, the smaller the problem.

CHAPTER 8: The 4 A's

> Face the problem, and start solving it.

> Communicate with others, but don't dump your problems on them.

> A problem isn't really a problem, unless you allow it to be. Appreciating your adversity can feel counterintuitive; however, it helps with your perception. Look at it as an opportunity.

> Good company and laughter don't permanently solve any problems, but it makes things more acceptable for a while.

> Take an audit of how you speak to yourself. Phrases like, "I want to give up and never try again" and "I'm a failure" fills your fading cup. Don't base your self-worth on one bad experience, and don't judge your character on negative feedback from an unreliable source. You flourish when you believe in yourself.

> Let your bad experiences lead you to good ones.

Attitude

Your mental attitude is something you can control outright, and you must use self-discipline until you create a positive mental attitude. Your mental attitude attracts to you everything that makes you what you are.

-Napoleon Hill

This is one of the most crucial areas where I feel you need to take audit. According to Carol Dweck, attitude can be broken down into two mindsets: growth and fixed. Your attitude is the lens through which you perceive the world. It's the gamechanger. It's what feeds your feelings, which then lead to your actions/behaviours and creates your destiny. What is your attitude? Does life happen through you or to you?

Abraham Lincoln said, "Most people are about as happy as they make up their minds to be". You actually have a choice about how you feel if you take audit of your attitude. Now, don't get me wrong. We're all fallible as human beings, but often we can get caught up in doing rather than being. Remember to check in with yourself. If you're engaging in stinking thinking due to spending too much time listening to yourself rather than talking to yourself, then you need to do something about your attitude.

My mentor, Dallas Lyons, once taught me a three-word combination that changed my perspective. It should be taught over math in school, as it will get you much farther in life. Those three words are, "I get to".

If you approach any obstacle this way, suddenly your attitude is optimistic rather than pessimistic. It may take a little while to get to the unconscious competence layer, but it's worth it. An attitude of gratitude will serve you better in life and elevate you higher than your constant negative thoughts. So if your ANTs are dominating you, then you should do a check-up from the neck up.

Napoleon Hill stated that "Tolerance and an open mind are practical necessities of the dreamer of today". He said this nearly a hundred years ago. Every successful person throughout history was a dreamer, and every dreamer has to have a vision, from Martin Luther King to Steve Jobs. In order to be your highest self, you must have an open-minded attitude.

Your attitude is influenced by your belief system, which is what you say when you talk to yourself. You shouldn't let a negative thought take root in the heart, as when that happens, it becomes a belief. If your belief affects your attitude, what is your perception of the world? What is your attitude to failure? How do you perceive other people around you?

CHAPTER 8: The 4 A's

Perhaps you think that people driving too slowly are idiots, or if they're going too fast, they're erratic or a nutter. Your self-perception can be thwarted, but it's your attitude that humbles and influences your feelings, which lead to your actions (behaviour). You need to work on your attitude, as it determines how successful you will be. It's what dictates if life is happening through you or to you.

As Shad Helmstetter shows us, there are layers to our belief system that then dictate your attitude.

The first of these is negative acceptance, which consists of statements like "I can't" or "I won't". Lucky enough for me, I was brought up to understand from a young age that this wouldn't help me get through life. If you find you're making these statements to yourself, you should know they do not serve you.

The second layer is recognition, such as "I should" or "I could". In this instance, you must finish the sentence to turn it around. This is levelling up your auditing abilities to really maximise your attitude and progress from a fixed to a growth mindset.

The third layer is where your subconscious is being moulded, and you identify with the words "I never" and "I no longer". What you're doing is contributing to the neuroplasticity of the brain to build a better future. This is where the fixed mindset blends with the growth mindset. Making the decision to change is key to your future actions, as again, attitude drives feelings, which drives your actions.

The fourth layer has to do with positive self-talk. It's where you finally deal with your fears and doubts, so instead of thinking "I can't", your mind is instead filled with the self-belief that you can do it.

The final layer is universal affirmation. This can be either a positive or negative belief, which is a fixed mindset you don't want challenged. An example of this is how doctors were used in advertisements for cigarettes back in the day. We were also told loading up on carbs and starch-like products was the staple of a good diet and that eating low-fat was healthy. As a result, you might have had the attitude that you were healthy, and any evidence to the contrary was rejected, even with clear scientific evidence to the contrary. It can be difficult to change a fixed mindset.

In my personal reality, I've found that loving adversity and being present with the person you are now, is the key to attitude building. As previously shared, when I was filled with negative emotions, my perception wasn't beneficial to my health, my future or those around me.

We all have tests in life, but it's how you get back up to conquer another day that constitutes a winning attitude. To give you some perspective, your issues dictate your emotions. If you're reading this book, then you're more than likely part of the top percent of the world who's fortunate enough to be literate, have access to electricity, running water, and know where your next meal is coming from. Real problems consist of not knowing how you will feed your family and living in favelas/slums or being in Panguna, Papua New Guinea, where your human rights are cast aside. Your land is taken from you, and you're excavated and exploited.

Due to your perception and getting into your own head, you often don't get perspective about the beauty of life, how good you have it and also how far you've come. Attitude is essential for your future. If you see the world in a radiant light, then you will attract more positivity, more gracious people and get more from life. It's a mirror reflection of what

CHAPTER 8: The 4 A's

you choose your perception of reality to be. *Where the mind goes, energy flows.*

Life pushes you around, but you must learn to move on and gain wisdom, which is the application of knowledge. If you do not, then you foster a blame attitude, acting below the line. Your mind is a tool, so you must understand how to use it. It's malleable.

You're in control of your thoughts, habits, actions and destiny. I used to be consumed with past thoughts and feelings. It was part of my present identity. But now I know it was a lesson that triggered my purpose.

The past is history, tomorrow is a mystery and "the present" is a gift. What's done is done. It can't be changed. But you can rewire this memory. I recommend a specialist to help you, such as a psychologist, as they can educate you on your brain and its functions, as well as helping you understand how you can heal, be present and move forward. When you think your best days are in the past, then you're in a state of depression. It's important to ask yourself these questions:

- ✓ What will you do to let these things go?
- ✓ How willing are you to let these things go?
- ✓ What is your resistance level?

Suffering is a choice. It's the lens of your perception. But it can sometimes be rooted in being uneducated about how to deal with adversity. A tragedy doesn't have to define you. It can help you heal, so you can then heal others. I recommend taking audit of your environment, association and input. Are you surrounded by energy vampires or people who lift you up?

- ✓ When you take ownership of your attitude, you take ownership of your life.

- ✓ When you take ownership of your adversity, you take ownership of your life.

- ✓ When you take ownership of your accountability, you take ownership of your life.

- ✓ When you take ownership of your authenticity, you take ownership of your life.

CHAPTER 9
BOUNDARIES

Setting boundaries inevitably involves taking responsibility for your choices.

- Dr Henry Cloud & Dr John Townsend

CHAPTER 9: BOUNDARIES

In order to know who you are, I feel you need to set healthy boundaries. This doesn't mean you can't help other people as you progress into the third stage of interdependence, but you need to be there wholeheartedly for yourself, before you can be there for others.

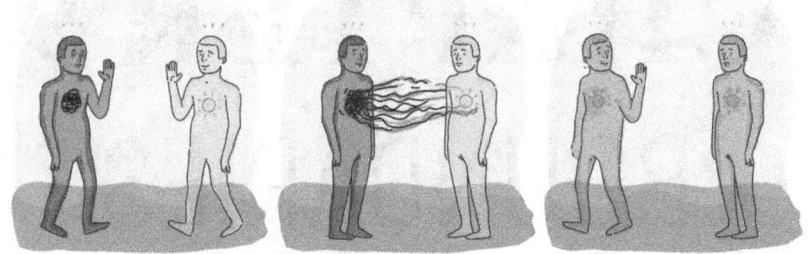

As you can see from the diagram, some people are energy vampires who leave you feeling depleted and dump their fuzz on you. Identifying these people and not giving them any more of your time, is a sign of being a healthy adult.

A healthy boundary enables you to grow. As a recovering people-pleaser addict myself, I've learned the hard way, but I'm now blessed to share my failures. You're the most important person on this planet. You're enough. Do you respect yourself enough that you can have a healthy life balance? Do you respect yourself more than you respect others?

One element of having boundaries is the preservation of your aims or goals. Often, family can impinge on your resolve when they communicate that "they know best". If you have no boundaries, you may continue through life trying to please them while jeopardising your own future, and ultimately, your fulfilment.

CHAPTER 9: Boundaries

Those who've adjusted to the mindset in *Rich Dad, Poor Dad* know how powerful perspective is. But if you have an unhealthy boundary, where you view your family's advice as your only choice, then this is an unhealthy boundary. Your family has an emotional investment in you, but they are not you. Understand that you are your own person, and you're enough. This is the premise of people-pleasing. You're trying to make everyone happy, but you're not owning your own consciousness.

If somebody gives you advice, you must have a healthy boundary to question it by asking yourself, *Would I trade places with this person?* If not, then do you have the kind of healthy boundary system that will thank them for their advice and move on?

One of my mentors taught me that you must "fix the root, to fix the fruit". You should question what fruit this person has to offer and how much you'll let them have a say in the choices you make. As I said, wisdom is the application of knowledge, and knowledge is potential power, so be conscious of your boundaries.

> *Boundaries are your mental, physical, emotional, and spiritual parameters that help us distinguish what is our responsibility and what isn't.*
>
> -Noble and Kathy Gibbens

> **Time**
>
> *Love yourself enough to set boundaries. Your time and energy are precious. You get to choose how you use it. You teach people how to treat you by deciding what you will and won't accept.*
>
> -Anna Taylor

A huge boundary aspect is time. Another one of my mentors taught me that life is like a loo roll. At the beginning, you pull off as much as you can with not a care in the world. You live young and free, with little worry about the future. But as the loo roll continues to get used, your perspective shifts. You realise it's not as thick as when you started and begin using each sheet sparingly.

Time is one of the biggest commodities in the world, and when you give it to somebody, you're investing in them seeds to be sown.

I used to live frivolously with my time, but now I have healthier boundaries. Often a healthy way to prioritise your time is to set expectations when you meet someone. By letting them know what you anticipate from the time given, you will both enjoy being around one another.

Positive thinking doesn't help you take action. It remains in thought. By taking a leadership position, you change your perspective and can thus solve your problem.

Often you can think that family is your value, so you have to give them all of your time, but if this is true, then you would find ways to leave a legacy for them.

CHAPTER 9: Boundaries

You have the same twenty-four hours per day as everyone else. You may spend eight hours sleeping and another eight at work, but how do you spend the rest of your time? People seem to have the delusion that they have all the time in the world, so they may waste it. However, by understanding the true value of time, and using it to your full advantage doing things and being with people who are worthwhile, it will help you flourish.

> **Money**
>
> *Daring to set boundaries is about having the courage to love ourselves, even when we risk disappointing others.*
>
> -Brené Brown

Another aspect of being a people-pleaser/caretaker is lending out your self-equity. You have to learn to open the till of life and put your hands in there.

How often do you audit the amount you lend/pay to loved ones? Is there a friend who owes you money? As a people-pleaser, I would lend friends money and have since learned where I didn't have healthy boundaries.

My empathy went out to these people, and I wanted to share with them. Now that I have a healthier relationship with money, I understood that you act your wage, not your age. A new pay rise or doing well doesn't mean an incremental increase in expenditure, but the opposite. I jeopardised my own self-equity, which resulted in unnecessary stress on my end.

Poverty is a fear that can be front facing for some. I'm not saying to never trust. However, if somebody owes you money, then you must say,

"I understand the position you're in, but until you pay back what you owe, I'm not able to lend you more. I hope you understand my point of view". This is setting a boundary.

If they push you, then repeat your boundaries. "This money that you want to borrow is my own, and I need it to fit in with my own priorities, so I can't lend you more".

If they become aggressive or unwilling to respond, then you will need to say, "I'm not going to tolerate the way you're talking to me, so I will not engage in a conversation with you, until it's safer to do so". Your next actions are then up to you.

If they say, *"You don't understand"*, this is a wall they've built, and they're covering up for something. Don't fall into this trap. I recommend *pausing, and then playing*. For example, you can take a deep breath and say, "All right, I'm trying to be empathetic with you, but I feel we're not resolving this, so please refrain from asking me again".

If you lack boundaries, then you could be compliant or an avoider, or both at the same time. Being compliant means you jeopardise your own energy due to shouldering too many responsibilities. Avoiders withdraw and tend to not ask for support from others.

Compliant avoiders suffer from reverse boundaries, so therefore they have no boundaries when they need them and then have boundaries when they don't. As somebody who has worked hard on this issue, I can say that all of the information I'm sharing has come from my own practice and discovery. A lot of this is rooted in childhood, but it's never too late to start growing into a healthy adult, which means having healthy boundaries.

CHAPTER 9: Boundaries

Altogether, boundaries are the key to learning who you are. You have to be able to sit with yourself with minimal stress, but also give yourself enough time to reflect on who you are. Tim Ferris says that, "More than eighty percent of the world-class performers I've interviewed meditate in the morning in some fashion". I believe that meditating is a great tool to becoming healthy and also to de-stress. If you win in the morning, then you win the day. Why would you not take your brain to the gym to worship yourself by putting yourself first?

CHAPTER 10
THE HEALTHY ADULT

I've always believed that if you put in the work, the results will come. I don't do things half-heartedly because I know if I do, then I can expect half-hearted results.

- Michael Jordan

CHAPTER 10: THE HEALTHY ADULT

There are three power parts to becoming a healthy adult. They are:

- ✓ Self-Awareness
- ✓ Self-Compassion
- ✓ Belief

Healthy Adult is a term coined by ACT, in regard to your higher self. All of the information I've given you up to this point consists of the ammunition and tools you need to arm the healthy adult. But first, you must understand what it is.

"Healthy adult" is not a punitive term. It's where you can take a step back and regulate your schemas/modes by recognising when they're maladaptive.

As a healthy adult, you're able to adjust your modes, and through adaptation, glide into the next stage. Being a healthy adult means you experience never-ending growth during your journey, knowing you will not be great at anything when you first start. Values are the skeleton of the healthy adult. However, the downside is that you can get hooked on your values.

The second part is that you need to be adaptable and *stay present*, so you can grow and change. Then your workability will increase, and you move forward.

CHAPTER 10: The Healthy Adult

The third piece to the puzzle is emotions and expansion. These two go hand in hand, as expansion works to increase your personal bandwidth. This covers all areas, whereas in cognitive psychology, your brain only has the capacity for certain kinds of information. This process of emotional bandwidth and expansion can be the most daunting part, as ugly truths can come out.

When people make accusations, they're projecting their issues onto others. Expansion is what evolves you into the person you're destined to be. Accepting accountability is another aspect of growth, as nobody is able to make you feel a certain way. By remaining objective about your feelings and then labelling them, you will be elevated.

As previously discussed, we all have ANTs. Mine used to be, "You're such an idiot". But when you realise this is the critical adult, the unreliable narrator, and that this is just one of your modes, you can unpack where this thought is coming from. Then you're able to acknowledge it, connect with it and move on by utilising the validating and accepting techniques above. You are not the voice, but the one who hears it. You are in control. It may be difficult, but it will give you the battle scars to become the healthy adult. The use of thought tools will also help.

A great technique to help empower you is the maturation process below:

- ✓ Live in days.
- ✓ Work in months.
- ✓ Plan in years.
- ✓ Think in half-decades.
- ✓ Dream in decades.

Another concept is *the courage to be disliked*. There are two objectives for behaviour: to be self-reliant and to live in harmony with society.

One part of EQ is social engagement. It backs up the idea that you have the consciousness that people are your comrades. In order to be a healthy adult, certain criteria have to be in balance. Martin Seligman talks about the PERMA effect.

- ✓ **P**ositive emotions
- ✓ **E**ngagement (flow state)
- ✓ **R**elationships
- ✓ **M**eaningfulness (Where you're part of something that's bigger than your being, which attracts a lot of people to group sports.)
- ✓ **A**ccomplishment (Not falling in love with the destination but striving to be your best.)

The second caveat for the healthy adult is that three of these additional features must be present:

- ✓ Optimism
- ✓ Self-Esteem
- ✓ Vitality
- ✓ Self-Determination
- ✓ Resilience
- ✓ Positive relationships

CHAPTER 10: The Healthy Adult

With these in balance, you're the definition of well-being. You're literally a being who is well. The healthy adult is somebody who is thriving, flourishing and fulfilled in life.

Anxiety and depression can typically be characteristics of unfulfillment. Anxiety is living in the future, and depression is living in the past, so you must be in *the gift that is the present.* Fear is something every human deals with, but it's a travel companion you must accept throughout life as you search for pleasures in your world.

Achievement is a never-ending journey. Success is rented, and every day you must pay. A great way to view this is to look at "how far you've come". This is a reflection tool, without letting it hook you into the past. You must choose an inside-out move. Feelings are the language and energy of the body. Thoughts are the language of the mind and emotion is energy in motion.

Your brain only weighs three pounds, but it's the storage device for your subconscious, which leads to your self-being. It's a network of tens of billions of neurons and electrochemical switches called neurotransmitters, which send messages to your brain. These are then sent out as thoughts. Mastering your thoughts and acting congruent to them means being a healthy adult.

Know that we humans are imperfect, and that's what makes us perfect. We're forever growing and building on who we are. You won't get there by comparing yourself with others but comparing yourself against yourself, knowing the person you could be and how far you can push yourself. Setting healthy boundaries will help you be content.

By using your tools and unhooking from your stubborn beliefs, you're able to embrace healthy moves forward. You're being kind to yourself, knowing you have standards. Your path to being a healthy adult is your guide to understanding your values.

> **Self-Awareness**
>
> *In our personal lives, if we do not develop our own self-awareness and become responsible for first creations, we empower other people and circumstances to shape our lives by default.*
>
> -Stephen Covey

Self-awareness is the foundation of the healthy adult, especially in regard to growth and change, as you need to be self-aware to know your being.

Tash Urick's research shows that having self-awareness creates better performers, influencers and communicators. It essentially creates better leaders.

What is self-awareness to you? Is it:

- ✓ Strengths and weaknesses
- ✓ How your actions affect others
- ✓ Knowing your triggers
- ✓ Understanding how your words and actions affect others

CHAPTER 10: The Healthy Adult

- ✓ Knowing where your perspective comes from, especially in regard to your past
- ✓ Recognising what to say when you talk to yourself
- ✓ Being aware how people perceive you

Self-awareness is defined as "the will and skill to understand yourself and how others see you". This is powerful if it's harnessed correctly.

Ninety-five percent of people believe they are self-aware, but only ten to fifteen percent of us actually are.

Amy Morin, in her book *13 Things Mentally Strong People Don't Do*, talks about self-awareness as "identifying when you blame external circumstances and other people for how you think, feel, and behave". Morin goes on to advise, "Take a close look at the people you are devoting your time and energy toward." This touches on the idea of *association*. Through your neuro mirrors, you adapt as a social being by copying those around you, but may not even be aware of it.

If you're saying, "You make me feel ___", this is where extreme ownership comes into play. Extreme ownership is a mentality. It's pure accountability. You must be your own champion not by being hypervigilant, but being aware of your presence. Through martial arts, I've become more in tune with my body, my awareness and how to be settled in my own skin. Like with everything, starting is difficult. However, there are three seasons: seed time, progression time and harvest time. Let your self-awareness grow and be self-empathetic, and you shall see the changes

Without self-awareness, you will struggle to identify your natural abilities, tendencies, boundaries, strengths, weaknesses and purpose.

This is done through knowing your emotions and being in the moment. You relate it to your feelings, what you're thinking, what you're saying and what you're doing. It's being able to understand how the other person's/event's/group's actions or words may affect your feelings and how to express yourself appropriately.

If you're not self-aware, you won't be able to understand yourself or recognise what's going on inside of you. Meditation has taken my state of self-awareness to a newfound level, due to connecting with my breath. At the end of the day, we breathe to stay alive. We are not taught about being connected with our breath. We don't think about it, yet it's what keeps the body operating.

Self-Compassion

Focus on remedies, not faults.

– Jack Nicklaus

Throughout this book, there's a fair amount of "self" references, and I feel that self-compassion is one of the quintessential attributes you must harness that will enable you to know yourself. It's the healthy adult elevator. You may be similar to me, where you have high standards, and the critical voice may tell you that you're not good enough to meet them. Sending love to your inner being is key to living a fulfilled life and knowing who you are. We are not our thoughts, but we are our words. There are some techniques to growing self-compassion, so let's start by defining what it is. First of all, it's by no means a cop-out to increase apathy, but to be kind and loving to yourself.

CHAPTER 10: The Healthy Adult

Kristin Neff defines self-compassion as being composed of three main components: self-kindness, common humanity and mindfulness.

No single human gets through childhood without scars. However, you can't live a life of lies, where you're the victim and constantly feel sorry for yourself. But on the other hand, you shouldn't be too self-critical. Through acknowledging your own suffering and responding kindly, you can minimise feelings such as fear, anxiety, failure, frustration, disappointment and sadness.

As Dr Russ Harris says, we must first acknowledge the pain. Know that you're in a state, label it, feel it, understand what it is and then learn how to unhook. The previous techniques I've spoken about will arm you to defuse harsh self-talk. We're evolving into a new age of humans. Our brain's job is to solve problems. If you're in pain, your mind tries to figure out ways to stop it and evolves to solve the problems. Your job is to assess whether your mind's solutions are effective. What will be the next evolution? In the past century, we've seen electric vehicles, mobile phones and people sent out into space, and we keep accelerating at an exponential rate.

At the root of self-compassion is *kindness*. What is kindness? To me, it's performing acts directed towards harmony and peace. Acting with kindness is essential, as it's the glue that holds everything together. You must recognise that we're not software or robots, but souls having an earthly experience. Acknowledging the pain and sending kindness is part of self-compassion.

The next evolution is *acceptance*. You must accept your feelings, emotions and thoughts. An eye-opener for you may be to take audit of your coping mechanisms during times that emotions and thoughts overwhelm you.

Do you drink alcohol, especially on the weekend, to supress your life, because you're working five days and living as society has told you to? Do you smoke cannabis to deal with some of those thoughts and to relax or get creative? Do you reach for the muffins, chocolate and lollies, because you're not happy with the shell that you're in? Do you sniff cocaine to fit in, to up your feelings, so that you enter a euphoric state and then continue to pursue the high? These escapism tactics are how you distract your life away. It stints your progress in learning about who you are. When you practice accepting these feelings, thoughts, memories and sensations instead of participating in self-inflicting acts, that is a kindness in itself.

The next step to building self-compassion is to *validate* what's going on in your body. Your mind tells you that you shouldn't feel a certain way. Are you getting your validation from watching television shows? Are you being told by society that your feelings are wrong? You need to have healthy boundaries in place to let you know that your feelings are acceptable. That you're okay just as you are.

Through self-talk, you level yourself up. Tell yourself, *It's okay to feel/be/think this way right now*. And remember to be careful of being critical, as this is when you're most sensitive.

One of the biggest points I want to offer is, *Don't compare yourself to others*. Comparison is the root of destruction. It's the thief of joy for everyone on their own path. Unfortunately, due to the rise of social media, we're constantly comparing, and this billboard of opinions is there any time, day or night, luring you in. But you must remember that nobody else on this planet gets the privilege to enjoy today like you or gets the opportunity to smile at yourself in the mirror and send kindness to yourself like you do. Nobody else in the world has the honour of

CHAPTER 10: The Healthy Adult

living a day in your shoes. Remember that you're on your own path, so be kind to that path. It's the small, seemingly insignificant habits, steps and rituals that, done daily and over time, will lead to radical results. At the end of the day, everyone starts somewhere, and the best time to begin is now!

Surrounding yourself with like-minded people is the key to your success. You're a product of your associations. Make sure you have people you feel are safe to talk to about what you're going through. These are true friends. Remember that your problem is not unique, so send love, not shame. Send light, not shadow, and connect with others. Your pain is not a sign of weakness but that you're a human being who is alive!

Self-compassion can take time, but it pays to be kind to yourself. At the end of the day, you need to be your biggest fan and know who you are, so in the end, you win.

> **Belief**
>
> *You have to expect great things of yourself before you can do them.*
>
> -Michael Jordan

The last part of being a healthy adult is *belief.* A belief system is a big dream backed by quality decisions + consistent action, which creates certainty. Your belief carries you. Do not make the mistake of judging your belief system by what you've received.

Belief-killers are doubts, fears, questioning results and the committee of *they*. Belief-builders are faith, hope, commitment and diligence. I'm not talking about the religious connotation of faith, but the true meaning of believing in the unknown. In terms of PERMA (page 102), knowing the destination is giving yourself time to succeed.

You have to change what you say about yourself. Cut the belief system (BS) down to a growth opportunity.

Every successful person in the world once started out believing in an idea, such as Jeff Bezos with selling books, Jack Ma with Alibaba and Michael Jordan with playing basketball. What are you dreaming about? A dream not written down is a fantasy. Once it's written down, then you create actionable steps. With consistent action, you give rise to certainty, which brings your dream to fruition. You're not created for the fun of it. Believe in yourself, as you are your biggest fan. You have to love yourself to believe in yourself. I genuinely feel you must have the clarity of vision for belief, but who am I to judge? Go out there, and prove your belief system is in control.

Explode the TNT today, not tomorrow. You're never too old to start anything. Want proof? Have you ever seen the man behind Kentucky Fried Chicken? Colonel Saunders? His name was Harland David Sanders, and he was sixty-two when he franchised his secret recipe to a local restaurant. Do you think he had a BS that questioned him? Of course. But he beat that, didn't he? Your potential is whatever you want it to be. They don't teach you this in school. You must own your belief system.

Belief is something you have to work on, as self-belief comes from your own lion heart and owning your actions. If you had a troubled upbringing, that's okay. Your parents didn't whisper belief into you, but you now have ownership of your life. You can go out into the world and build your belief system.

CHAPTER 10: The Healthy Adult

Belief, behaviours and values are the sauce for cognitive congruence. You already understand values and behaviours, as they come from your feelings and emotions, so let me expand on the idea of belief. Your BS is the key to your pandora of dreams. You will never rise above your expectations, so expansion is a contributing factor to prosperity. Your belief system is built from knowing your why/purpose + decisions + action + certainty. You can't judge your belief system on what you've received but what your mind can conceive.

Through knowing your three P's (chapter two), you're ready to take on your belief. You know your personality. You get you and what you radiate to the outside world through your poise. Your purpose is who you are destined to be, the dream that you showed up on the planet to produce. Your guide, the healthy adult, illuminates the dark, leads you to the truth and rises to the purpose poise personality of your own reality.

> *Most of your unhappiness in life is due to the fact that you are listening to yourself rather than talking to yourself.*
>
> -Dmartyn Lloyd-Jones.

THE FINAL WORD

You are the way you are, because that's the way you want to be. If you really wanted to be any different, you would be in the process of changing right now.

- Fred Smith

THE FINAL WORD

Now you're armed with knowing who you are. Congratulations on reaching this point through navigating introspection and reflection. You know what you need to live a prosperous life, and I believe in you.

Subconsciously and fundamentally, feelings of unworthiness, people-pleasing and a desire to get a good performance rating can drive the decision-making processes. This is why it's so key to be conscious about your being, while connecting with yourself and flourishing. Being self-aware will drive you, and self-compassion will nurture you with accountability, adversity, authenticity and attitude.

I want you to be free and to harness certainty. But this process will take time, so practice self-compassion. Consistency is key. Learning who you are is essential to life, but so is kindness. Give yourself time to grow.

What are you accepting? How are you using your time, and where are you going to end up? As the days turn into weeks, the weeks into months, months into years, and years into decades, every grain of intention amplifies your personality and reality. Time promotes you or exposes you. Hunger is the fuel of accomplishment.

We are advancing at a truly exponential rate. Less than a hundred years ago, we had the last public execution in France by guillotine (1939), the first bananas came to Norway in 1905 and the internet was born in 1983. The Stone Age didn't end because people ran out of stones. It ended because people kept learning, improving and adapting.

The Final Word

We are now in the information age. Just over 120 years ago, there was the very first scientific study of anger, and the first study on empathy was introduced in the 1920s. What will the next hundred years look like? We now consume three times as much information as we did in the 1960s. It's within your capacity to develop skills that will enable you to thrive. As Seligman has taught us, the golden standard of human beings is to flourish. Entering flow state is optimum living.

Are you living with honour?

Taking responsibility for your life is your choice. Excuses are like exits along the road of success that lead you nowhere. Taking the exit is easy, but it gets you off-track. It's impossible to have excuses and success. Conquering the temptation to give up becomes the commentary for successful people. If you want to do something, take responsibility for it. Finding an excuse may alleviate the pressure, but it doesn't help your future.

You determine your reputation by deciding who and what you are by keeping your vision in mind, even when you're having an amazing time, which happens through the equilibrium of you mind, body and spirit/being. What you don't transform, you transfer. Suppression is the easiest way out, but to live nobly, with honour and grace, is a rarity and the sign of an elevated soul.

I've learned that you have to be your authentic self, as that dark image you've been conjuring is behind you. It's fictitious. Don't believe your perception that the world is really bad if you step out as yourself. Live as a healthy adult by having a purpose, knowing your personal reality, having great poise with an upbeat attitude, and being accountable to yourself and your actions.

You weren't born just for the fun of it. Dreaming big requires you to stretch. You're not designed to blend in but to stand out. What can impinge on your ability to see it through, is fear. The moment you realise that fear is *False Evidence Appearing Real*, you can harness the truth. Fear kills dreams more than failure ever will. It's a false emotion. Knowing that a thought can't beat a thought, what action will you take to stand out and live the life you're meant to live? Your vision is your mission.

Life isn't meant to be fair. Your problems are not unique. You don't get what you hope for, you get what you deserve. You have choices as to how you respond to disappointments. Life isn't waiting for the storm to pass but learning how to dance in the rain. Millions of people saw the apple falling from the tree, but it was Newton who asked why. What will you question? What will you be consistent with? Who are you?

This book has been a pleasure to write and a great way to share my learnings. I hope it's impacted you. Thank you for investing your time. I appreciate and believe in you.

ABOUT THE AUTHOR

I'm Alexander Eduardo Gil, and I'm part of the Gil heritage that goes back to the Fifteenth Century north-eastern part of Spain that wasn't conquered by the Moroccans, who ruled Spain for six-hundred years. I don't look Spanish, and nor do I look Welsh, some could argue. My lineage is mostly hard-working, middle-class people.

My mum's side are people of the valleys in Wales and go back to farmers. So, who am I? I'm a values-driven, aspirational, optimistic chap whose many life tests are my testimony. I'm a caring man with a growth mindset; a global citizen. I've invested hugely in personal development and believe the best investment you can make is in yourself. Take the time to grasp this information, and let it talk back to you. I hope as you read this, that your own voice reads it back. And if you find this isn't the case, you might want to talk to someone about it.

ACKNOWLEDGMENTS

I would like to take this time to thank all of the people I've had the opportunity to interact with. You've helped write this book.

To my parents for bringing me into the world and giving me everything you have.

To my grandparents on both sides, for the lessons, values and love you've instilled in me. I'm nothing without my connections.

I owe a lot of my guidance to Dallas and Lisa Lyons and your belief in me. You have mentored me to be the best version of myself.

To the McKenna family for your hope, anteambulo ways, guidance and heart. Helen, Peter, Dominic and Karina, thank-you.

To Noble and Kathy Gibbens for your light, whole-heartedness and support. Your 'Eq" course is an elevator for every human and needs to be a subject taught in school.

To Emily, Leah and Jennette for your patience, guidance and sharing of knowledge. I am forever indebted to you both.

To Lily Hair, for your support throughout the tough times, great times and for your creativity.

To Robert Cutler and Joel Steggall for your input, support and being chief error handlers.

Acknowledgments

To my friends, Valerio Vestita, Joseph Grimshaw, Jessica Tosh, Craig Kelly, Richard O'Toole, Catlin Jones, Forest Robinson, Braden Ippolito, James Rogers, Denise Ryan, Aimee Bingley, Rhys Evans, Catlin McLeod, Thomas Jones, Darbie Hill, Alex Brough, Annie Medwin, Stephen Sandhu, Ella Ackland, Josh Sole, Season Sutton, Timothy Bates, Daniel Canfield, and Olivia Frey.

To my beautiful editor, Caryn, for your hard work. To Narelle, for making this into a beautiful masterpiece, your patience and beauty.

I want to thank Ed Mylett, Darren Hardy, Jim Qwik, Daniel Goleman, John Maxwell, Gary Newell, Travis Bradberry, Jean Greaves, Stephen Covey, Urban Meyer, Simon Sinek, Robert Kiyosaki, Ryan Holiday, Dave Ramsey, James Clear, Spencer Johnson, Bob Burg, Jon Gordon, Brian Tracy, Brené Brown, Anthony Laye, Elka Whalan, and Jonice Webb. I have not met you yet, but your lives inspired me to put this together to add value to others.

Thank you.

REFERENCES

Melody Beattie, *Codependent No More*

Travis Bradberry, *Emotional Intelligence 2.0*

Dale Carnegie *How to Win Friends and Influence People*

Steven Covey, *The Seven Habits of Highly Effective People*

Carol Dweck, *Mindset*

Tim Ferris, *Tools of Titans*

Robert A Glover, *No More Mr Nice Guy*

Daniel Goleman, *Emotional Intelligence*

Darren Hardy, *The Compound Effect*

Dr Russ Harris, *The Happiness Trap*

Chad Helmstetter, *What to Say When You Talk to Yourself*

Napoleon Hill, *Think and Grow Rich*

Robert Kiyosaki, *Rich Dad Poor Dad*

Florence Littauer, *Personality Plus*

Amy Morin, *13 Things Mentally Strong People Don't Do*

References

Jordan Peterson, *12 Rules for Life*

Jim Qwik, *Limitless*

Dave Ramsay, *More than Enough*

Martin Seligman, *Flourish*

Dr. Seuss, *The Sneetches*

Simon Sinek, *Start with Why*

Simon Sinek *The Infinite Game*

Jonice Webb, *Running on Empty*

THE ULTIMATE LIST OF EMOTIONS TO HELP YOU IDENTIFY YOUR FEELINGS:

Absorbed
Abhorrence
Acceptance
Admiration
Adoration
Adrift
Aching
Affection
Afraid
Agitated
Agony
Aggravated
Alarm
Alert
Alienated
Alive
Alone
Amazed
Amused
Anger
Angst
Animated
Animosity
Animus
Annoyed
Antagonistic
Anticipation
Antipathy
Antsy
Anxiety
Apathetic
Apologetic
Appalled
Appreciative
Apprehensive
Ardor
Arousal
Astonishment
Astounded
Attachment
Attraction
Aversion
Awe
Awkward
Baffled
Bashful
Befuddled
Bemused
Betrayed
Bewildered
Bitter
Blessed
Bliss
Blithe
Blue
Bold
Bonhomie
Boredom
Bothered
Bouncy
Brave
Breathless
Brooding
Bubbly
Buoyant
Burning
Calm
Captivated
Carefree
Caring
Cautious
Certain
Chagrin
Challenged
Chary
Cheerful
Choked
Choleric
Clueless
Cocky
Cold
Collected
Comfortable
Commiseration
Committed
Compassionate
Complacent
Complaisance
Composed
Compunction
Confused
Courage
Concerned
Confident
Conflicted
Consternation
Contemplative
Contempt
Contentment
Contrition
Cordial
Cowardly
Crafty
Cranky
Craving
Crestfallen
Cross
Cruel

The Ultimate List of Emotions

Crummy	Disturbed	Excitement	Gratified
Crushed	Doleful	Excluded	Grateful
Curious	Dopey	Exhausted	Greedy
Cynical	Doubtful	Exhilaration	Grief
Defeated	Down	Expectant	Groggy
Dejection	Downcast	Exuberant	Grudging
Delectation	Drained	Fanatical	Guarded
Delighted	Dread	Fascinated	Guilt
Delirious	Dubious	Fatigued	Gung-ho
Denial	Dumbfounded	Feisty	Gusto
Derisive	Eager	Felicitous	Hankering
Desire	Earnest	Fervor	Happy
Desolation	Ease Ebullient	Flabbergasted	Harassed
Despair	Ecstatic	Floored	Hatred
Despondent	Edgy	Fondness	Heartache
Detached	Elated	Foolish	Heartbroken
Determined	Embarrassment	Foreboding	Helpless
Detestation	Empathic	Fortunate	Hesitant
Devastated	Empty	Frazzled	Hollow
Devotion	Enchantment	Free	Homesick
Disappointed	Energetic	Fretful	Hopeful
Disbelief	Engrossed	Frightened	Horrified
Disdain	Enjoyment	Frustrated	Hostile
Disgruntled	Enlightenment	Fulfilled	Humiliated
Disgust	Enmity	Furious	Humored
Disillusioned	Entertainment	Genial	Hurt
Disinterested	Enthralled	Giddy	Hyper
Dismay	Enthusiasm	Glad	Hysterical
Distaste	Envy	Gleeful	Impatient
Distracted	Euphoria	Gloomy	Incensed
Distress	Exasperated	Goofy	Indifferent

Indignant	Lighthearted	Nostalgic	Protective
Infatuated	Liking	Numb	Proud
Inferior	Listless	Obsessed	Psyched
Inspired	Lively	Offended	Pumped
Intense	Lonely	Optimistic	Puzzled
Interested	Longing	Outrage	Quizzical
Intimacy	Lost	Overwhelmed	Rage
Intimidated	Love	Pacified	Rapture
Intoxicated	Lucky	Pain Panic	Rattled
Intrigued	Lust	Paranoid	Reassured
Introspective	Mad	Passion	Receptive
Invigorated	Meditative	Pathetic	Reflective
Irascible	Melancholic	Peaceful	Regret
Ire	Mellow	Peevish	Relaxed
Irritated	Merry	Pensive	Relief
Isolated	Miffed	Perky	Relish
Jaded	Mirth	Perplexed	Reluctance
Jealous	Mischievous	Perturbed	Remorse
Jittery	Miserable	Pessimistic	Repugnance
Jocular	Mollified	Petrified	Resentment
Jocund	Mortified	Petty	Resignation
Jolly	Motivated	Petulant	Restless
Jovial	Mournful	Phlegmatic	Revolted
Joy	Moved	Pity	Sad
Jubilant	Mystified	Playful	Sanguine
Jumpy	Nasty	Pleasure	Satisfied
Keen	Nauseous	Positive	Scandalized
Lazy	Needy	Possessive	Scorn
Left out	Nervous	Powerful	Secure
Lethargic	Neutral	Powerless	Self-Conscious
Liberation	Nonplussed	Preoccupied	Selfish

The Ultimate List of Emotions

Sensual	Stunned	Trepidation
Sensitive	Stupefied	Triumphant
Serendipitous	Submissive	Troubled
Serene	Succor	Trust
Settled	Suffering	Twitchy
Shaken	Suffocated	Upbeat
Shame	Sullen	Upset
Sheepish	Sunny	Uptight
Shock	Superior	Vehement
Shy	Sure	Vexation
Sick	Surprised	Vigilant
Silly	Startled	Vindication
Sincere	Sympathy	Vindictive
Skeptical	Tenderness	Warmth
Sluggish	Tense	Wary
Smug	Terror	Weak
Snappy	Testy	Weary
Solemn	Tetchy	Welcome
Solicitous	Thankful	Woe
Somber	Thirst	Wonder
Sore	Thoughtful	Woozy
Sorrow	Thrill	Worry
Sorry	Timid	Wrath
Sour	Tired	Wretched
Speechless	Titillation	Yearning
Spiteful	Tormented	Zeal
Sprightly	Torn	Zest
Stirred	Torture	
Stressed	Touched	
Strong	Traumatized	
Stung	Tranquil	

Examples of schemas/modes are:

Emotional neglect, entitlement, mistrust, defectiveness/shame, abandonment/instability, dependence/incompetence, enmeshment/undeveloped self, insufficient self-control/self-discipline subjugation, approval-seeking, negativity/pessimism, self-sacrifice, emotional inhibition, unrelenting standards/hypocriticalness.

www.ingramcontent.com/pod-product-compliance
Lightning Source LLC
Chambersburg PA
CBHW071518080526
44588CB00011B/1480